THE FIVE WOUNDS OF JESUS

In Memory of
MADALINE MARY STAPYLTON
(1899–1992)

THE FIVE WOUNDS
OF JESUS

David H. Williams

GRACEWING

First published in 2004

Gracewing
2 Southern Avenue
Leominster
Herefordshire
HR6 0QF

© David H. Williams 2004

ISBN: 0 85244 620 9

Typeset by
Action Publishing Technology Ltd, Gloucester

Printed in England by
Antony Rowe Ltd, Eastbourne BN23 6QT

CONTENTS

ILLUSTRATIONS

ACKNOWLEDGEMENTS

Scripture quotations are from the *Revised Standard Version of the Bible*, copyright © 1946, 1952, and 1971, by the Division of Christian Education of the National Council of the Churches of Christ in the USA. Used by permission. All rights reserved.

Extracts from *Hymns Ancient and Modern Revised* are by permission of SCM-Canterbury Press, Ltd., Norwich; hymn 436 appears by permission of Continuum International Publishing Group. Extracts from the *English Hymnal* are by permission of The Oxford University Press and Continuum. An extract from its Office Book is by kind consent of Mount St Bernard Abbey. Extracts from *The Divine Office* appear by permission of A.P. Watt, Ltd., on behalf of the Hierarchies of England and Wales, Ireland and Australia.

The author is further indebted to the Principal of Ripon College, Cuddesdon, for permission to reproduce the Prayer of Richard Crawshaw; to the Banner of Truth Trust, Edinburgh for kindly consenting to the reproduction of extracts from *Daniel Rowland and the Great Evangelical Awakening in Wales* (1995) as well as from *Wesley and Men Who Followed* (2003); to the Society for Promoting Christian Knowledge for graciously consenting to the use of extracts from *Orthodox Spirituality* (1945), *John Climacus, The Ladder of Divine Ascent* (1982) and *Marked for Life* (1995). Extracts from Sr Penelope, *The Works of William of St Thierry* are used with permission of Cistercian Publications, Western Michigan University, Kalamazoo. Verses from the hymnology of William Williams (Pantycelyn) appear with the kind consent of Dr R. Brinley Jones. Quotations from Fulton Sheen's *Life of Christ*, are by permission of Doubleday, a division of Random House, Inc., and from Professor Duffy, *The Stripping of the Altars*, by consent of Yale University Press.

Diary, St Marian Faustina Kowalska, Divine Mercy in My Soul, © 1987. Congregation of Marians of the Immaculate Conception, Stockbridge, MA, USA. All rights reserved. Used with permission.

Details of all these works, and their authors, will be found in the Bibliography.

Every effort has been made to trace copyright, but sometimes this has proved fruitless.

Illustrations

Fig. 1: By permission of the Bodleian Library, University of Oxford (Arch. G. f.14), *Fig. 2*: Extract from the Poem of William Billyng, appears by permission of the Syndics of Cambridge University Library. *Fig. 3*: the Measure of the Wound of Christ, is taken by permission from Volume 30 of the *Journal of the British Archaeological Association* (1974). *Figs. 4, 8, 10 and 13* were kindly provided by Dr Madeleine Gray. *Fig. 8*: appears by permission of Lord Raglan. *Fig. 5*: the translation of the inscription on the Foxwist Memorial is the work of Mr John M. Lewis, MA, FSA, formerly of the National Museum of Wales. *Fig. 6*: the Coventry ring is taken from the volume of the *Gentleman's Magazine* for 1803. *Fig. 7*: the National Arms of Portugal are reproduced by permission of the Instituto dos Arquivos, Lisbon. *Fig. 11*: the photograph (National Monuments Record AA 52/2567) taken by the late C.J.P. Cave, appears by permission of the Friends of Winchester Cathedral. *Fig. 12*: kindly provided by Mr Brian Huseland. *Fig. 15*: photograph, by NADFAS; *Fig. 17*: Éditions Combier, which we have been unable to trace despite a painstaking search; *Figs. 18 & 19*: specially photographed by Fr Peter King, Cwmtillery.

Abbreviations

A and M Rev.	*Hymns Ancient and Modern Revised* (William Clowes, Ltd., 1972).
EH	*The English Hymnal* (Oxford University Press, 1933).

INTRODUCTION

In writing this short book, on a subject which has long been dear to my heart, I have not hesitated to give it an ecumenical flavour. In a country where the knowledge of God is limited to say the least, the more the Churches draw together the better they will fulfil the will of Christ, 'that the world may believe' (John 17.21).

I am very grateful to: Mr Ray Balfour of Norwich for substantial translation out of German, and for communicating to me the expertise of Professor Barbara Raw, who has herself kindly written to me; to Dr Dafydd Huw Evans, Dr Michael Siddons, M. Paul Bryant-Quinn and Mr Graham C.G. Thomas for drawing references to the Five Wounds in Welsh poetry and literature to my attention; to Dr Michael Siddons, FSA, Wales Herald Extraordinary, for heraldic references, and a copy of Thomas Percy's ballad; and to Mr John Goodall, FSA, for leading me to the Inventories of Henry VIII.

Dr Madeleine Gray very kindly lent me photographs of Welsh examples of the Five Wounds from her collection; the Dean of St David's, the Very Revd. Wyn Evans, FSA, and Mr Tom Longford drew my attention to a carving in St David's Cathedral; the Revd. Terry Mart made me aware of stained glass from Llangystennin, whilst the Revd. John Angle (North Cadbury), and Fr Peter King (Six Bells), very kindly supplied me with photographs of images in their churches. Mr Brian Huseland, whom I met by chance in St Tudno's on the Great Orme, took and e-mailed to me fine pictures of the roof boss there. Lord Raglan readily assented to the inclusion of an image in his house.

I was much helped by clergy, churchwardens and others, who met me at their churches: the Revd. R.J. Hughes at Llanbeblig; Miss Sheila Crosby (twice) at St Tudno's on the Great Orme; the Revd. Canon R.H. Griffiths at Llan-rhos; the Revd. J.M.T. Carlyon, and church workers, at Bedwellty, and the Revd. V.C.T. Tucker and Dr Colin Jones, at Gresford, whilst Llandudno Museum provided helpful information.

Not least, I owe the pleasing appearance of this book to Mr Tom Longford and Jo Ashworth of Gracewing.

David H. Williams
Aberystwyth, Ceredigion, SY23 1LR
1 March 2004
St David's Day

CHAPTER ONE

THE SCRIPTURAL BACKGROUND

In the Psalms and the prophetic books of the Old Testament are sayings which, even if not intentionally meant to do so, foreshadow the Passion of Christ and his wounding for our redemption. This is not surprising given that, to use modern theological jargon, the writings of the Old Testament form part of our 'salvation history'. The prophesy of the wounds of Christ comes plainly in the book of Psalms – 'They have pierced my hands and my feet' (22.16), and in Zechariah's response, 'They shall look on him whom they have pierced' (12.10). Unknowingly, the Psalmist and the prophet foretold the action of the Roman soldiers very many years later:

> When they came to Jesus and saw that he was already dead, they did not break His legs. But one of the soldiers pierced His side with a spear, and at once there came out blood and water.
>
> (John 19.33–34)

Yet, as a well-known hymn points out, it wasn't only from His side, but from 'His head, His hands, His feet', that 'Sorrow and love flowed mingling down'.

It was, of course, we who wounded Christ – by our sins, by our frequent departures from purity and honesty of life. It wasn't just the Jews who betrayed Him nor the

Roman soldiers who nailed Him to the Cross; what they did, they did as it were in our name. It was we who stabbed Him in the back, as Zechariah foretold:

> If one asks Him, 'What are these wounds on your back?' He will say, 'The wounds I received in the house of my friends'.
>
> (13.6)

Or, to put it in the words of the Negro spiritual:

> Were you there when they nailed Him to the tree;
> Were you there when they pierced Him in the side?

Isaiah, too, prophesied that 'He was wounded for our transgressions' (53.5), but it was a wounding with a purpose, and so St Peter wrote: 'By His wounds, you have been healed' (2.24). And of course we continue to wound Him, whenever we turn our back on Christian principles, whenever our love for Our Lord grows dim, and whenever we deny Him by actual wrongdoing. Because He is timeless, without beginning or end, our wounding is in a real sense a cause of His Passion. Perhaps the greatest wounds of all, are the ones we are trying to heal, the wounds in the Church, the division and disunity in His mystical Body here on earth. Yes,

> He had no form or comeliness
> that we should look at Him,
> And no beauty that we should desire Him,
> He was wounded for our transgressions.
> He was bruised for our iniquities.
>
> (Isaiah 53.2,5)

Some writers see also in the pages of the Hebrew Scriptures the foretelling of the living water of eternal salvation – when Moses struck the Rock and the Israelites had their thirst quenched, and the concept of sheltering in the wounds of Jesus – as when the Lord said to Moses, 'While my glory passes by, I will put you in a cleft of the rock', and when Elijah hid in a cave until he heard 'the still small voice of calm'. The window opened in Noah's Ark has been seen as a symbol of the piercing of the side of Christ.

In the account of the Resurrection given by St John in his Gospel the sacred wounds of Christ come to prominence, for when Jesus, on the evening of the first Easter Day, stood among the fearful disciples and 'shewed them His hands and His side' (John 20.20), it was His way of reassuring them that He had conquered death, and that they had nothing to fear for He was with them still. 'Then the disciples were glad' (John 20.20). His hands and His side bore the marks of the spear and the nails, they were marks by which He could be recognised as the Risen Lord indeed, but much more than that they were the battle-scars of His victory over evil. In a book given to me in 1959, by the first pupils I taught for Advanced Level Geography, Bishop Fulton Sheen put it well:

> This was the first gaze of the disciples upon a risen and glorious Lord. These nail prints, His pierced side, were the unmistakable scars of battle against sin and evil ... if the scars had been removed, men might have forgotten that there was a sacrifice and that He was both priest and victim.
> (*Life of Christ*, London, 1966)

At first the disciples that Resurrection Day evening 'were startled and frightened, and supposed that they saw a spirit' (Mark 24.37), so Jesus used His scars as a mark by which they could recognise Him; it was His way of calming them down. Even so, 'they still disbelieved for joy'. They had clearly forgotten, or never completely grasped, all He had tried to tell them in the preceding months and years.

Those scars of His wounds are a reminder to us today, that those who follow Christ will not always have an easy time. Far from it for those, who in every age and even now, have known persecution on account of their Christian faith and practice, sometimes severe – even to the point of death. For the Christian Way is not meant to be a smooth road, the life of the baptised who are faithful to the promises made for them in their infancy will not always be one of ease and leisure. Rather, like St Paul, they might have 'to bear on their body the marks of Jesus' (Galatians 6.17).

Suffering, in one form or another, will frequently be the lot of those who cling to Christ and reject 'the devil and all his works'. Sabine Baring-Gould recounted the story of St Martin of Tours:

> One night the devil appeared to St Martin crowned with gold and gems, and in a magnificent vestment sparkling with jewels. 'I am come in judgement', he said, 'Adore me.' 'Where', asked Martin, 'are the mark of the nails, the piercing of the spear, the crown of thorns? When I see the marks of the Passion I shall adore the Lord.' The devil disappeared.

There was one disciple, 'Thomas, one of the twelve, called the Twin', who was not with the others when Jesus came:

> The other disciples told him, 'We have seen the Lord.' But he said to them, 'Unless I see in His hands the print of the nails, and place my finger in the mark of the nails, and place my hand in His Side, I will not believe.' Eight days later ... Jesus came and stood among them ... and said to Thomas, 'Put your finger here, and see my hands; and put out your hand, and place it in my Side; do not be faithless, but believing.' Thomas answered Him, 'My Lord and my God!' Jesus said to him, 'Have you believed because you have seen me? Blessed are those who have not seen and yet believe.'
>
> (John 20.24–29)

A passage which shows that the wounds of Christ were substantial ones, particularly the spear gash in His Side, large enough for a hand to be placed within, and well paraphrased by Tisserand:

My piercèd side, O Thomas,
  see;
My hands, my feet I show to
  thee;
Not faithless, but believing
  be.

No longer Thomas then
  denied
He saw the feet, the hands, the
  side;
'Thou art my Lord and God',
  he cried.

> How blest are they who have not seen,
> And yet whose faith hath constant been!
> For they eternal life shall win. Alleluya!
> (*A and M Rev.*, n. 130, v. 6–8)

Jesus in this further appearance not only satisfied Doubting Thomas, but more importantly left an enduring message for us of the need for faith and trust in the teachings of Scripture and the Church, and of utter confidence in the power and the promises of Christ. The lesson Thomas learnt, is one for us as well.

> Kneel before His wounded feet,
> Touch His hands and Side,
> Leave your doubting and
> Believe the Son of Man.
> (*Mount Saint Bernard Office Book*)

The scene within the closed doors of the house where the Twelve were assembled attracted the attention of St John Chrysostom, who was at pains to point out that although Jesus appeared in visible form this did not mean that His Body was a corruptible one, and that His appearance was solely to shore up the weak faith of the twelve, not for self-glorification. In his *Homilies on the Gospel of Saint John*, written somewhere about AD 390, Chrysostom writes:

> It is worth enquiring how an incorruptible Body shewed the prints of the nails, and was tangible by a mortal hand ... this marvel was shewn that the Resurrection might be believed ... on this account He arose ... so after the Resurrection when we see Him with the print of the nails, we will

no more say that He is therefore corruptible. For He exhibited these appearances on account of the disciple.

For all humanity, there will come a Day of reckoning for, as the Book of Revelation puts it: 'Behold, He is coming with the clouds, and every eye will see Him, every one who pierced Him', for we are those 'Who set at naught and sold Him, pierced and nailed Him to the Tree' (*A and M Rev.*, n. 51). For those who, in this life, have turned their backs on Jesus and their neighbour, this Last Day will be an awful occasion, a bitter sight. The early 12th-century Celtic poet, Elidir Sais (*c.* 1195–1246), put it well:

> He will shew the scourges, and all His wounds,
> And the nails, and the blood, and the Cross;
> 'I did all this – and you, what have you done?'
> Says Christ, King of heaven.
> (*Penguin Book of Welsh Verse*)

For us all, the last day that really matters is the last day of our earthly lives and the state of our souls at the moment of our death, for that will determine whether we greet the eventual Second Coming with joy or with trepidation. For the faithful Christian, the sight of the glorified yet pierced Christ will be an enduring moment of utter bliss:

> Those dear tokens of His Passion,
> Still His dazzling Body bears,
> *Cause of endless exultation*
> To His ransomed worshippers,
> *With what rapture*
> Gaze we on those glorious scars!
> (*A and M Rev.*, n. 51)
>
> O *joy all joys beyond*,
> To see the Lamb who died,
> And count each sacred wound,
> In hands, and feet, and side.
> (*EH* n. 496)

The sacred wounds of Christ have entered into eternity:

See! He lifts His hands
above,
See! He shews the prints
of love
(*EH* n. 143)

Behold His hands and
side,
Those wounds yet visible
above,
In beauty glorified
(*EH* n. 381)

The fact that the resurrected and glorified body of
Christ showed quite unmistakably the five wounds, was a
sign that He was indeed the same Christ who had suffered
and died for us. It was one of the post-Resurrection
appearances which, taken together, made the disciples
realise that 'It is the Lord' (John 21.7). When He called
Mary Magdalene by name, when He indicated where the
disciples should lower their net, when He broke bread in
the house at Emmaus, and when He pointed out His
sacred wounds, He was demonstrating vividly that He was
the real Jesus they had known so well.

More than that, it is a sign for us that our glorified
bodies in the next life will express our total personality in
our human existence. Whatever the nature of our 'spiritual body', it will be the real you and the real me; we shall
know others and be known; for St Paul assures us that He
'will change our lowly body to be like His glorious body'
(Phil. 3.21).

All that is in the future. The message of the Five
Wounds is that we must have a concern *in this life* for the
wounded nature of our lives and those of others, for
the wounds in the side of the Church – its disunity, for the
wounds in society – the widespread practice of abortion,
the millions facing near-starvation. When our hearts are
moved for them, when we pray for them and give alms to
help them, then in a minimal but real way we share in the
suffering of the Wounded Christ.

CHAPTER TWO

THE EARLY CHURCH AND THE
MEDIEVAL SCENE

Early Christian writers saw the piercing of the side of Jesus as rich in symbolism. Hippolytus (*c.* 170–236) talked, in his *Discourse on the Holy Theophany*, of Jesus 'who is pierced in the side, and restores the side of Adam' – emphasising that the gashing of Christ's side by the spear put right the sin introduced by Eve who had been fashioned by God out of Adam's side. Later writers emphasised the wound in the side as being the sacred opening from which the Church and its Sacraments came forth – though St Augustine did not neglect the other wounds of the Lord:

> Behold, I beseech Thee, Lord, the wounds in thy hands and thy feet.
> For lo in thy hands Thou hast written me,
> read thine handwriting and save me.

Words echoed by Charles Wesley in the lines of his hymn describing Jacob's encounter with the angel:

> I need not tell Thee who I am,
> My misery or sin declare;
> Thyself hast called me by Thy name;
> Look on *thy hands*, and read it there!
> (*A and M Rev.*, n. 343)

St John Chrysostom (347–407), commenting on the

text in St John, 'at once there came out blood and water', writes plainly:

> ... the one was a symbol of baptism, the other of the mysteries [i.e.: the Eucharist] ... it is from these two that the holy Church has been born ... by baptism and the mysteries ... it was from His side, then, that Christ formed the Church, as from the side of Adam He formed Eve ...

And, of course, it is because both 'blood and water' flowed out of the side of Christ that, even today, a little water is mingled with the wine at the offertory at every Eucharist.

St John Chrysostom went on to emphasise the Real Presence, that the very Christ is indeed truly received at Holy Communion though masked by the outward signs of bread and wine:

> When thou approachest to that awful Cup, thou mayest so approach, As drinking from the very Side.

St Augustine (354–430), commenting on the same Gospel, and using such text of the Scriptures as was available to him, gives the same teaching, adding that the opening of a door in the side of Noah's ark prefigured the piercing of Jesus's side:

> ... the Evangelist ... does not say, 'pierced His side' or 'wounded' or the like, but *opened*; that therein might be thrown wide the door of life, from which the Sacraments of the Church have flowed out ... in first announcement of this ... Noah was bidden to make a door in the side of the ark, by which should enter the living creatures that should not perish in the flood, by which creatures the Church was prefigured ...
>
> The first woman was made out of the side of the man as he slept ... the second Adam with bowed head slept upon the Cross, that thence might be formed for Him a wife, even that [the Church] which flowed forth from His side as He slept.

As a medieval poem put it:

> Holy Church took first foundation,
> When Longius' spear through mine heart ran.

Theodoret (*c.* 393–458), Bishop of Cyr in Syria and for long a friend and admirer of Nestorius, despite his reservations about Mary as *Theotokos* (Mother of God), was orthodox in following John Chrysostom and others:

> His side was opened ... to reveal the fountain of life ... with its double stream. One stream gives us new life in the baptistry ... the other feeds those who have been reborn at the divine table.
>
> (*Divine Office, III*, p. 409)

In some Carolingian manuscripts the Wound in the side is equated with the life-giving baptismal font, whilst Gougaud points out that 'in all ages the Wound in the Side was pre-eminently the object of veneration'. He quotes tradition as asserting that the spear pierced the right side of Christ's body and that, because of this, at the fraction during the Mass of the Five Wounds a small part of the right-hand side of the host was detached, and the chalice was placed not behind the host but on the right of it.

Another early Christian writer, roughly contemporary with Augustine and John Chrysostom, St Peter Chrysologous (400–450), saw the wounds of Christ as efficacious signs of his great love for us:

> These nails do not pierce me with pain; they pierce me more deeply with love of you. These wounds do not draw groans from me, rather they draw you into my heart.
>
> (*Divine Office, II*, 561)

Or, as Isaac Watts much later put it:

> From His head, His hands, His feet,
> Sorrow and love flow mingling down.
>
> (*A and M Rev.*, n. 108)

Several centuries later, thoughts similar to those of the Early Church entered into Cistercian spirituality. St Bernard (1098–1153) saw the sacred wounds as being like crevasses in which the faithful could shelter, a theme much to the fore after his time in the *Anima Christi*, with its supplication: 'Within thy wounds hide me', and, much later still, in Augustus Toplady's hymn:

> Rock of Ages, cleft for me,
> Let me hide myself in thee.
>
> (*A and M Rev.*, n. 210)

St Bernard also thought of the wounds as being a source from which the Christian might draw spiritual food, and as being the means of God showing His love and mercy for us. He wrote:

> Where is a safe stronghold for the weak to find rest, if not in the wounds of the Saviour … They pierced His hands and feet and opened His side with a lance, and through these *clefts* I may 'suck honey out of the rock and oil out of the flinty *rock*', which is 'to taste and see that the Lord is good'. … The nail that pierced became for me the key that opened the door so that I might see the will of the Lord … The nail cries out, the wound opens its mouth to cry that truly God is in Christ reconciling the world to Himself … Where, more clearly than in your wounds, does it shine out that you, Lord, are meek and humble and abounding in mercy? (*Divine Office*, *I*, 451–52)

How well Mrs C.F. Alexander put it, that Irish Anglican hymn-writer with a flair for transforming complex theological matters into [plain] easy-to-understand but dignified verse, without losing any of the meaning of the doctrines concerned nor in any way lessening the truth conveyed:

> Lift up Thy bleeding hand, O Lord,
> Unseal that cleansing tide;
> We have no shelter from our sin
> But *in Thy wounded Side*. (*A and M Rev.*, n. 88)

In the writings of William of St Thierry (1085–1148), St Bernard's confidant and soul-mate, comes the equation – to the fore in modern times – of the Wound in the Side with the Sacred Heart of Jesus:

> I want to see and touch the whole of Him and, what is more, to approach the most holy wound in His side, the portal of the ark [the Church] that is there made ... Lord, whither do you draw those whom you embrace and enfold, *save to your heart* ... Blessed the souls you have hidden in your heart, that inmost hiding-place.
>
> (*The Works of William of St Thierry*, 1971)

Once again, we see the Church as issuing from the Wounded Side, and the concept of that Side as being a place where the baptised might take refuge.

Nor was thought on the spiritual importance of the Five Wounds confined to Cistercian circles. The Benedictine St Peter Damian (*d.* 1072), like St Bernard later proclaimed a Doctor of the Church, taught that: 'Christ is pierced by a fivefold wound, so that we may be healed from the entry of vices, which reach us through the five senses'. The Dominican Bl. Henry Suso (*d.* 1366) was another churchman who emphasised the Five Wounds as 'signs of love'; out of reverence for them, he drank five times during each meal.

Throughout the Middle Ages, there were those who received visions of the Suffering Christ and of His Five Wounds. St Aelred (*d.* 1167) told of a Gilbertine nun, who 'saw Christ hanging on the Cross, affixed with nails, pierced by the lance, pouring out blood by five openings'. For St Catherine of Genoa (*d.* 1510), refused permission by her father to enter a convent, and enduring an unhappy marriage, a similar vision was the turning point of her life. Already very devout, Catherine was henceforth completely given over to penance and good works.

The leper St Aleydis, of the Cistercian nunnery of La Cambre in Belgium (*d.* 1250), received a like vision despite, or perhaps because of, being isolated for fear of infection from the rest of her community. (The fact that, for the same reason, she was not allowed to communicate from the chalice, is one of many pointers that at this stage Communion in both Kinds was universal).

Eton tells how 'Our Saviour appeared to St Mechtilde (of Helfta, *d.* 1280), and exhorted her often to shelter herself in the sacred wounds of His body. In His feet to place all her affections to be purified and cleansed; in the wound of His right hand all her actions to be perfected, in His left all her afflictions to receive ease and comfort, in the wound of His side her heart, that joined with His it might be set on fire with divine love'. Another example of the Wound in the Side as being equated with, or leading to, His Sacred Heart.

A Flanders mystic, St Lutgarde (*d.* 1246), transferred to the stricter enclosed life of the Cistercian nunnery of Aywières, following a vision of Jesus revealing to her the spear-wound in His Side, and telling her: 'Behold here, forever, what you should love'. Bl. Julian of Norwich (*d. c.* 1414), granted a similar appearance by Our Lord, described the Wound in the Side as 'a fair, delectable place, and large enough for all mankind that shall be saved to rest in peace and love'.

St Bridget of Sweden (born in 1302), whilst still very young, saw the Crucified Jesus saying to her, 'See, my child, how they have wounded Me'. The redoubtable Margery Kempe of Lynn, who probably knew and may have been influenced by Bl. Julian, told how she 'beheld His body ... fuller of wounds than ever was a dove-house of holes'.

Douglas Gray points out that in the later Middle Ages the arithmetically minded worked out the number of all Christ's wounds and even of the drops of blood He shed. (A chancel roof shield in Gresford Church displays a cross spattered with drops of blood). Estimates for the wounds varied, the most common being 5461, 5466 or 5475. A 15th-century British Library manuscript (Add. MS 37049) suggests 'five thousand, four hundred, sixty and fifteen', as does a Welsh verse in the poetry of Robin Ddu: '5475. hyny oedd rifnedi archollion krist' (5475. That was the number of Christ's wounds). Madeleine Gray rehearses the 'story of the woman "solitary and recluse" whom Christ told in a vision that the number of his wounds equalled the number of fifteen *Pater nosters* said daily for a year' (15x365=5475).

The popularity of devotion to the Five Wounds by the 15th century saw speculation as to their size (*Fig. 3*). One Book of Hours suggested that the Wound in the Side measured some 2.5 inches in length and 1.2 inches in breadth. A representation of the measure of the Wound in the Side was supposed to have an indulgence granted by Innocent VIII (1484–1494). The shape of the wounds differs frequently between one representation and another. As for the current location of the lances that inflicted the wounds, Nuremberg, Paris, Rome and elsewhere, all make claim to them.

As has been noted, reference to the Five Wounds occurs quite often in medieval verse of a religious nature. Douglas Gray quotes from a 15th-century poem:

> O Jesu, let me never forget Thy bitter passion,
> That thou hast suffered for my transgression,
> For in Thy blessed wounds is the very school,
> That must teach me with the world to be called a fool.

John Lydgate (1370–1451) concluded his ode, *As a Mydsomer Rose*, by comparing the Five Wounds to five wells (of mercy and of grace):

> It was the Rose of the bloody field,
> Rose of Jericho, that grew in Bethlehem;
> The five Roses portrayed in the shield,
> Displayed in the banner at Jerusalem.
> The sun was eclipsed and dark in every [part],
> When Christ Jesus five wells [bound] unclosed,
> Towards Paradise, called the [red] stream,
> Of whose five wounds print in your heart a rose.

One of the most notable poems in honour of the Five Wounds was that written by, or perhaps copied by, one William Billyng. Axon suggests that it appears to be of the early 13th century, and copied in its present form – on an illuminated 2³/₄ yard long roll – around 1400 to 1430 (*Fig. 2.*). It commences:

> Cometh nere ye folkes temtyd I dreynes
> Wyth the drye dust of thys erthly galle
> Resorte anon wythe alle your wysyaes
> To the V stremes flowen over alle.

Mention of the Five Wounds is a regular occurrence in Welsh verse throughout the Middle Ages. To quote but one example, by Iolo Goch (*c.* 1320–1398):

Pum archoll I'n arfoll ni,	Five wounds to receive us,
Pum aelod y pum weli,	The five members of the five wounds,
A'n rhoi yn iach, ein rhan oedd,	And to make us well, our fate it was
A wnâi Siesus yn oes oesoedd.	Did Jesus suffer for ever and ever.

Llywarch Brydydd y Moch also referred to 'the piercings of Christ, bringing five ages from slavery', whilst Guto'r Glyn (1440–1493) referred to 'the form of God, full of wounds' and, at the Last Day, 'fear of the wound that slew Him'.

There is some evidence in Welsh verse that, to quote Glanmor Williams, people 'swore by His wounds and took His name in vain'. This appears to be the meaning of words written by Gruffydd Llwyd (*c.* 1380–1410):

Mynych y guneir, eurgrair oll,	Often, wholly fine treasure,
Amherchi dy bum archoll.	Are your five wounds disrespected.

In England, certainly by Shakespeare's day – and as in that playwright's *Hamlet* and *Henry IV, Part I*, the wounds of Christ were sometimes taken in vain in a form of blasphemy. Swear words included 'Odsblood' and 'Zounds'; the first relating to His Blood that was shed, the second to the Wounds He bore.

Nor did the Elizabethan Age exclude a consideration of the Passion, even though actual devotions to the Five Wounds were largely a thing of the past. Nicholas Breton (1545–1626) perhaps penned the lines frequently attributed to Mary Sidney, Countess of Pembroke (1555–1621):

> To see the feete, that travayled for our goode,
> To see the handes, that brake that livelye breade,
> To see the heade, whereon our honor stoode,
> To see the fruite, whereon our spyrite fedd.
> Feete pearc'd, hands bored, and His heade all bleedinge,
> Who doth not dye with such a sorrow readinge.
> (*A Poem on Our Saviour's Passion*, London edn, 1862)

CHAPTER THREE

LITURGY AND ART

Glimpses only of the later devotion to the Five Wounds of Jesus may be traced in Britain prior to the Norman Conquest, in that certain antiphons of the medieval Good Friday liturgy can be traced back to the Anglo-Saxon prayer book, the *Book of Cerne*, whilst the Ælfwine Prayer-book has prayers to be said before a crucifix. From the 13th century onwards, prayers in honour of the Five Wounds become commonplace in Books of Hours. They were made popular perhaps by the fame of the stigmata of Francis of Assisi, and by their usage by other saints, like St Clare – who had the 'prayer of the five wounds' read to her on her deathbed in 1223.

St Clare used verses from Psalm 102, addressing the first verse to the wounds of the feet, the second to the wound in the side, the third to the wound of the left hand and the fourth to the right hand. Her prayers can be summed up in a few words they contained: *Vulnera quinque Dei sint medecina mei* ('The Five Wounds of God are my healing'), a motto that often latched on to later repre-sentations of the wounds.

The late 13th-century *Preces Gertrudianae* were typical of such supplications:

... I kiss the wound of thy left foot, in expiation of all the sins that have been ever committed in thy whole Church by thought or desire or intention ...

... I kiss the wound of thy right foot, for all the omissions made in thy whole Church, in good thoughts, in holy desires and pious intentions ...

... I kiss the wound of thy left hand, in expiation of all the sins of word and of deed, committed by the whole world ...

... I kiss the wound of thy right hand, in satisfaction for all the negligences in thy whole Church in useful words and good works

... I kiss the wound of thy most sacred side, beseeching thee that thou wouldst impart for the increase of its [the Church] everlasting bliss, the merits of all thy most holy life and conversation ...

Some of the prayers to the Five Wounds were very long; late-medieval orations of forty-eight and fifty-four lines are known, but an indulgence could be obtained for reciting a much shorter verse: 'Pardon and mercy, my Jesus, by the merits of thy sacred Wounds'.

Most people could not avail themselves of the prayers available to the educated classes. They were encouraged to honour the Five Wounds by reciting daily the Lord's Prayer five times and, later, the Hail Mary as well. Duffy quotes the will of a London mercer who desired five poor men to kneel every feast day at his tomb and repeat five *Paters* and *Aves* in honour of the Five Wounds. In 1927, Gougaud noted that in some Catholic countries bells were rung on Fridays before or after midday to remind the faithful to recite five *Paters* and five *Aves* in honour of the Five Wounds.

Prayer to the Five Wounds reached its apogée in the liturgy. A Little Office of the Five Wounds was known to Saint Clare whilst, also in the 13th century, the Thuringian monastery of Fritzlar had a metrical office honouring the same. From the same century the Dominican rite had a feast of the Wound in the Side, kept on the very day (the Friday after the Octave of Corpus Christi) that was later to be observed as the Feast of the Sacred Heart. Fritzlar Abbey kept by the 15th century a Feast of the Five Wounds; this spread in popularity and, as at Mayence in 1507, was also kept on the present day assigned to the Sacred Heart. The Cistercian Order kept it on the fifth Friday of Lent.

Devotion to the wounds of Jesus was also shown by the five consecration crosses incised on altar mensas – though altars are known with fewer or more than five, and the five wounds were also, and still are, remembered by the insertion each Holy Saturday of five incense grains into the side of the paschal candle.

It was the provision of propers for the Mass of the Five Wounds (equated by Duffy with the late medieval Jesus Mass) that set the seal of ecclesiastical approval on this devotion. There were other Passion Masses in the medieval Church – of the Face of the Lord (his ill-treated countenance), and of the Crown, Lance and Nails (the instruments of the Passion). The Mass, *Humiliavit*, the *missa de vulneribus Christi*, one tradition (legend rather) had it, was composed by St John the Evangelist, and revealed by the Archangel Raphael to Pope Boniface in the opening years of the 14th century. A more reliable source, the Dominican missal of 1519, has the Mass composed by Pope Boniface and confirmed by Innocent VI who attached indulgences to it. That missal prescribed that five candles be lit at the Mass of the Five Wounds.

The collect apart, the Mass survived into modern times as the Votive Mass of the Passion. The Epistle came from Zechariah with its telling words: 'the wounds I received in the house of my friends', and the Gospel from St John included his words: 'one of the soldiers pierced His Side with a spear'. After the gradual came a sequence; indeed, several appropriate ones were written.

Tradition had it, as recounted in a Heidelberg manuscript, that if the Mass of the Five Wounds was said five times for a departed person his soul would be released from purgatory. The exhibition catalogue of the recent *Images of Christ* exhibition at the National Gallery in London suggested that it was the Mass said at funerals, whilst Duffy points out that medieval testators might specify votive Masses other than the Requiem as part of their mortuary provision.

Philip ab Hywel of Llan-soe in Monmouthshire (*d.* 1534) and Gwenllian uch Res ap Jankyn of Abergele in Denbighshire (*d.* 1550), both made financial provision in their wills for five Masses of the Five Wounds. Philip made provision in perpetuity for five such Masses on each anniversary of his death; Gwenllian made her bequest even during the Protestant-minded reign of Edward VI. Duffy cites a Greenwich widow (in 1496) and a York metalworker (of 1516) as doing the same for the day of their burial.

The Collect from the Mass of the Five Wounds went thus:

> O Lord Jesus Christ, who came down to earth from the bosom of your heavenly Father, and washed away our sins by shedding your precious blood and enduring the five wounds on the tree of the Cross; we humbly ask you, that on the judgement day, we may be found worthy to hear those words, *Come, you blessed*, who with the same God, the Father and the Holy Spirit, lives and reigns for ever.

Testators might also leave bequests for the poor in honour of the Five Wounds. An alderman of London, Richard Gardener (1490), left 10d. for five poor men in this respect and for five poor women in honour of the Five Joys. In 1519, Dame Thomasine Percyvale bequeathed 5d. a week to be given to five poor householders in the parish of St Mary Woolnoth [London] in honour of the Five Wounds of Our Lord.

Such evidence that we have for Masses and charitable offerings in memory of the wounded Christ dates mostly from the 15th and early 16th centuries but, much earlier, the knights on the First Crusade (1096–99) had been told to make five charitable offerings 'on account of the Five Wounds of the Lord'.

Duffy points out that the fivefold symbolism of the

wounds was ubiquitous, even where the link with them was not made explicit, as in the Somerset will of 1471 which instructed the executors to give 'to 5 poor men 5 gownes, and also by an hoole yere next ensuying my decease 5d'.

Another London testator, and a former Lord Mayor of the City, Edmund Shaa, bequeathed in 1497 no less than sixteen gold rings engraved with 'the well of pity, the well of mercy and the well of everlasting life, and with all other images'. These were equated in late medieval thought with the Five Wounds.

Billyng's poem (referred to above) is accompanied by a figure of Christ as Man of Sorrows, and refers to the wound in the right hand as the well of mercy, in the left hand as the well of grace, in the heart (or side) as the well of life, in the right foot as the well of pity and in the left foot as the well of comfort (*strength*). The analogies may have stemmed from the prophecy of Isaiah: 'With joy you will draw water from the wells of salvation' (12.3).

To quote Lydgate again:

> At wells five, liquor I shall draw,
> To wash the rust of my sins quickly,
> I mean the wells of Christ's wounds five,
> Whereby we claim of merciful pity.

Such gold rings are known from other sources, and one (perhaps of the mid-15th century) was found in 1803 in a Coventry park (*Fig. 6*). It is inscribed on the inside with Latin verses, commencing with the catch-phrase of the Five Wounds, *Vulnera quinque Dei, sint medecina mei*. It reads: 'The Five Wounds of God are for me a medicine; the holy Cross and Passion of Christ are for me a balm; Caspar, Melchoir, Balthasar, ananizapta, tetragramma-ton'. This looking for the protective qualities of the Magi is still evidenced each New Year on the door lintels of many houses in Central, Eastern and Northern Europe, where the date of the year is marked in chalk with a cross and the initials, C (or G or K). + M. + B.

Other personal effects to display the wounds of Christ included pendant crosses, like that bequeathed by Maud, Countess of Cambridge (*d.* 1446) which had 'four great pearls and one ruby in the midst', representing the Five Wounds. Sir Brian Tuke (*fl.* 1540) wore on a chain a gold cross showing Christ's wounded hands and feet with the Crown of Thorns in the centre. Henry VIII's inventory, drawn up following the monarch's death in 1547, included two tables ornamented by the Five Wounds; the one by 'threads of venice gold upon flat gold', the other had the wounds 'embroidered upon black satin'.

In churches a common way of displaying the Five Wounds was by means of a shield having the gashed Sacred Heart in the centre between two pierced hands above and two feet below. Such shields – showing in Tudor times the equation of the Wound in the Side with the Sacred Heart – occur on roof ceiling bosses (as in St Stephen's cloister in the Palace of Westminster – built between 1526 and 1529), on brasses and memorial wall-plates (like that commemorating Richard Foxwist (*d.* 1500) at Llanbeblig, Caernarfon (*Fig. 5*), on bench-ends (as in the church of North Cadbury, Devon; *Fig. 15*), and on medieval sepulchres and chests (as those in the churches of Coety in Glamorgan and Bedwellty in Gwent; *Figs. 9, 10*). A wood carving of the stigmata (perhaps of the 15th century) also appears on a roof cross-tie beam at St Tudno's Church, Llandudno (*Fig. 12*).

At Froyle in Hampshire and Sidmouth in Devon, the church windows include shields showing five almond-shaped cuts dripping blood, each surmounted with a golden crown, and bearing the inscription: 'Wel of Wisdom, Wel of Mercy, Wel of Everlasting Lyf, Wel of Grace, Wel of Gudly Comfort'. Common are representations, as at Bowness-on-Windermere, of the Crucifixion with angels swooping down to hold chalices to catch the Precious Blood from each Wound. In Llandyrnog church glass (Denbighshire), the seven sacraments emanate from the wounded Side.

The Five Wounds have been employed on several banners and emblems. Alfonso of Portugal, in gratitude to Christ for his victory over the Moors at the Battle of Ourique (1139), placed the Five Wounds on the coat of arms of his new kingdom. There they remain today (*Fig.* 7). The Wounds are depicted by pieces of red cloth sewn on to the white linen crown of the Bridgettine nuns and on the cloaks of their lay brothers.

Attachment to the Old Faith and traditional ways saw the Five Wounds become the badge worn on the chests and the colours of the rebels of Yorkshire in the Pilgrimage of Grace (1536). Bishop Latimer (of Worcester, 1535–1539), preaching on the Epistle for Trinity 21 (Ephesians 6.10–20), said: 'I hear they wear the Cross and the Wounds before and behind'. At much the same time (1537), the parsh of St Keverne in Cornwall commissioned a banner depicting the Wounds.

Bishop Grindal of London said of the later Rising of the North in 1569: 'The rebel army had on their colours the Five Wounds'. The banner was borne by the aged Richard Norton of Conyers Norton, and so Bishop Thomas Percy's ballad went:

> The Norton's ancyent had the cross
> And the five wounds Our Lord did bear.

Footnote: One must take as spurious, but indicative of growing devotion to the Five Wounds in the latter Middle Ages, the legendary letter (known in Welsh as *Llythyrdan Garreg*) said to have been written by Our Lord and found under a great stone at the foot of His Cross, advising us to fast on five Fridays of the year in remembrance of the Five Wounds.

CHAPTER FOUR

MODERN TIMES

In continental Europe, devotion to the Five Wounds did
not cease with the passing of the Middle Ages; it has to a
degree re-emerged in Britain and it has spread to the
Americas. Amongst several confraternities which have
emerged in the Roman Catholic Church for the greater
veneration of the Five Wounds was one backed by a
bishop of Eystadt with approval from Innocent XII
(1691–1700).

Congregations named after the Sacred Heart have
included the Picpus Fathers, of whom Father Damien of
Molokai was a member. The traditional habit of their
priests and brothers incorporates both Sacred Hearts. The
desert hermit, Charles de Foucauld (1858–1916), also had
the Sacred Heart sewn on to his cloak. The Knights of the
Holy Sepulchre (founded by the papacy in 1868) bear on
their white cloaks a red cross with four smaller crosses in its
angles, representing the Five Wounds.

A few mystics have continued to receive visions of the
wounded Christ, and some religious on profession have
coupled the Five Wounds with their name in religion,
whilst clerics and laity have written and composed prayers
concerning the Wounds – as those in *The Inner Court: A
Book of Private Prayer*, published by Burns Oates in 1924.

In the second half of the 16th century, there were
several calls to the faithful to dwell upon the sacred

wounds of Christ. The *Second Book of Homilies* – finalised in 1571, and published in England on royal authority to combat illiteracy amongst some clergy and to ensure orthodox teaching – in the 'Second Sermon on the Passion' (*Appendix 1*) saw our redemption as 'purchased unto us by vertue of Christ's bloody Wounds'.

Across the Channel, devotion to the Five Wounds figured, but did not loom large, in the *Spiritual Combat* of Lorenzo Scupoli (1529–1610), a Clerk Regular of the newly established Theatine Order, and in the *Introduction to the Devout Life* of St Francis de Sales (1567–1622) who placed great reliance on Scupoli's work. The *Spiritual Combat*, a book I used to read a lot during National Service in Germany – the new English edition of which had just been given me by Marjorie Burnett, the inspiring senior Catechism assistant at my boyhood church (St John the Baptist, Newport) – invites us to meditate on Christ's agony upon the Cross:

> [Meditate] how when the Lord hung on the hard wood with no other support but the nails, His most sacred wounds were enlarged and aggravated with unspeakable pain by the weight of the body as it pressed downwards.

And Scupoli reminds us of Christ's sorrowful Mother standing at the foot of His Cross:

> How much the sufferings of His most holy Mother grieved Him. And these sorrows of hers themselves renewed the inward wound of her blessed Son, and His most blessed heart was wounded as if by so many arrows inflamed with love.

Whilst St Francis de Sales offers, as an antidote to Sadness, the advice to:

> Embrace the crucifix, kissing the hands and the feet, raising your voice to God in words like these, 'My Beloved is mine, and I am His'.
>
> (Song of Solomon 2.16)

St Francis also, in one of his letters to St Jane Frances Chantal, foundress of the Visitation nuns, written to her in 1604 on her widowhood, suggested she find solace by 'casting yourself, not vehemently but gently, into the Saviour's Wounds'.

Modern visionaries have included a lay Visitation sister of Chambéry in Savoy, Mary Martha Chambon (1844–1907), who, from 1866, received frequent visions of the Crucified Christ giving her His sacred Wounds to contemplate. A lifelong mystic, she died in 1907 after much suffering. It is said that she received her first vision of a bleeding and wounded Christ, when only five years old, during the Adoration of the Cross on Good Friday. Her Mother Superior kept a chronicle of her life which was published in 1923, and sold widely. The next year, the Vatican granted an indulgence to those who said the prayer Mary Martha asserted she received from the Lord:

> Eternal Father, I offer Thee the wounds of Our Lord Jesus Christ to heal those of our souls.

In Poland, Sister Maria Faustina Kowalska (1905–1938), through whose testimony the recent devotion to the Divine Mercy has been spread, tells in her *Diary*:

> Once I was summoned to the judgement seat of God. I stood alone before the Lord. Jesus appeared such as we know Him during His Passion. After a moment, His wounds disappeared, except for five, those in His hands, His feet and his side.
>
> (*Diary*, para. 36)

Sister Maria Faustina was by no means the only religious favoured by divine revelations to encounter a degree of hostility from her peers. On 25 January 1938, she wrote in her diary:

> A certain sister is constantly persecuting me for the sole reason that God communes with me so intimately, and she

thinks that this is all pretense (*sic.*) on my part. When she thinks that I have done something amiss she says, 'Some people have revelations, but commit such faults!'. She has said this to all the sisters and always in a derogatory sense, in order to make me out as some sort of oddity.

(*Diary*, para. 1527)

Speaking from personal experience, and not doubting that Our Lord has favoured those He has marked out with direct revelations, might it be that both in the medieval period and today some visionaries have received their messages (or in some cases hallucinations) during diabetic hypoglycaemic attacks? One night recently, when my blood sugar level was very low and I was lying in bed, I became very confused. I thought I was back on a fleeting visit to Caldey Island (where I served as Guestmaster in the abbey from 1983 to 1987). I saw two new young monks, one slightly bearded. They said the Abbot was coming across to see me. I awoke wondering whether this was a message that I should return to Caldey! I find, that as one recovers from such states of near collapse, everything appears in a very different light from usual.

A notable priest's housekeeper was Anna Maria Gallo (1715–1791), daughter of a harsh Neapolitan father. At the age of sixteen, she refused an arranged marriage and instead became a tertiary of a Franciscan Third Order, that of St Peter of Alcantara. She took for her name in religion that of Sister Mary Frances of the Five Wounds of Jesus Christ.

Accounts of her life differ. The *New Advent* web site suggests that on Fridays, especially in Lent, she felt in her body the pains of the Passion but received no visible stigmata. Others suggest that she had bleeding both from the head (a Crown of Thorns effect) and the other wounds. One Dean Pascal Nitti wrote: 'I have seen them, and like the Apostle St Thomas, inserted my finger in them. The wounds were right through her hands'.

Another holy nun to take the sacred wounds into her

name at profession was a Scottish girl, Margaret Sinclair
(1900–1925), born of humble origins in Edinburgh and
noted in her youth for her piety. She became, in 1923, a
Poor Clare Colettine extern sister at Notting Hill in
London, taking the name Sister Mary Francis of the Five
Wounds. In 1924, her abbess wrote that she was
admirable, and wanted nothing but the Will of God. Her
life was to be short-lived; she died from tuberculosis the
next year. There are currently moves to obtain her beati-
fication.

Amongst modern writers, Antonio Rosmini (1797–
1855), the founder of the Institute of Charity, whose writings in the past were subject to ecclesiastical censure,
approached the sacred wounds in a different light. In
writing of *The Five Wounds of the Holy Church*, he equated the
Wound in Left Hand of the Holy Church as being 'the Division between the People and the Clergy in Public Worship'.
He saw the Wound in the Right Hand of Holy Church as
being 'the Insufficient Education of the Clergy'; the
Wound in the Side as being 'the Disunion of the Bishops',
the Wound in the Right Foot as 'the Nomination of Bishops
being given up to the Lay Power', and the wound in the
Left Foot of Holy Church as 'the Servitus (or Enforced
Infringement of the Full Rights) of Ecclesiastical Property'.
No wonder he ruffled some feathers!

Antonio Rosmini can hardly have known of the anti-
episcopal and anti-Catholic sermon preached by James
Row o'Strowan, in St Giles Cathedral, Edinburgh, in
1638; the year when episcopacy was swept away from the
National Church. O'Strowan will have had no devotion as
such to the Five Wounds, but he used them as an analogy
in his severely critical approach:

> The Kirk o'Scotland is sorely wounded in her Head, in her
> Hands, in her Feet, and in her Heart. I. The Kirk o'Scot-
> land is Wounded in the Head in the Government. II. In
> her Hands, in the Discipline. III. In her Feet, in the
> Worship, and IV. In her Heart, in the Doctrine.

Today, there is an abundance of informative and devotional material regarding the Wounds on various web sites, whilst in the USA there is even a school dedicated to the Five Wounds, at San José in California. Regrettably, a film in very bad taste and entitled *Stigmata* appeared a little while ago on some screens in the USA.

Web sites aiding modern devotion to the Five Wounds include *stmaxmedia* giving a chaplet of the Five Wounds of Jesus (copyright – Doug McManaman); and *Catholic Paradise* outlining the Holy Rosary of the Sacred Wounds (web site created by Javier López). The *Last Days Ministries* web site quotes Thomas à Kempis: 'Take refuge in the Sacred Wounds of Christ'; while the *Holy Wounds Apostolate* web site is aimed at promoting devotion to Jesus Christ Crucified and Risen. It gives Marcel Gagne's 'My Week in the Holy Wounds of Jesus with Mary'.

A *Mystical Rose* web site tells us that the promises attached to words of Our Lord to saints like Gertrude, Mechtilde and Mary Martha Chambon are not part of the infallible teachings of the Church, and must not be viewed in a superstitious manner.

This web site also quotes the 'Annals of Clairvaux' as telling that Our Lord said to St Bernard that He had on His shoulder from carrying the Cross, 'a grievous wound more painful than the others', whilst the *Geocities* web site gives a prayer to the Shoulder Wound of Christ, in addition to prayers to the Five Wounds.

At least one recent writer, Maria Boulding, emphasises the assurance given us by the scars of victory of the Risen Jesus, in her *Marked for Life: Prayer in the Easter Christ* (1979). Talking of those who have been wounded, or been hard done by in this life in one way or another, she says:

> From the experience of His re-creative love I can look back without pain, guilt or shame. I bear the scars still, but they are very different from wounds. Scars can be honourable tokens of battle and of life fully lived. Jesus kept His and allowed the apostles to see and touch them; tradition says the body of the exalted and glorified Lord bears them for

ever. Transfigured and glorious they are tokens of His love for us. The same is true of our own healed wounds; in heaven they will be glorious and the cause of more joy. It begins to be true now, for I too am marked for life; my scars are tokens of His re-creative love, and as ever I must pray from where I am. My forgive-ness and my healed-ness are a prayer if I have the wit to let them be.

Bishop Fulton Sheen put well the message of Christian hope:

> The virile Christ is He who unfurls before an evil world the pledge of victory in His own Body – the scar-spangled banner of Salvation.
>
> (*Life of Christ*, 1956)

The Primate of Poland, Cardinal Joseph Glemp, in asking 'By what Paths has Providence led the Poles to Freedom', includes:

> The path of the *Cross and of Suffering*. The cemeteries, death-camps and calvaries cannot be forgotten. The Nation knew how to suffer – which signifies to come forth from *suffering victorious*, that is, to participate in the Resurrection.
>
> (*Poles – We enter now the Twenty-First Century*)

Fig. 1: Devotional card of the Carthusians of Sheen.

Fig. 2: Extract from William Billyng's Poem (*c.* 1400–1430).

Fig. 3: The Measure of the Wounds of Christ (15th century).

Fig. 4: Llangystennin glass, Co. Caernarfon (*c.* 1500). A pierced hand
points to the Wounded Side.

Fig. 5: The Foxwist memorial brass, Llanbeblig Church (1500). The brass shows Richard Foxwist, a notary of Caernarfon, holding a shield depicting the Five Wounds as he died. The opening verse reads: 'Richard Foxwist, in whom the glory of writing outshone many, is here trodden by foot. Thy year, O Christ, was 1500 in the Father's light, when he expiring holds Thy five wounds.'

(Translation, J.M. Lewis)

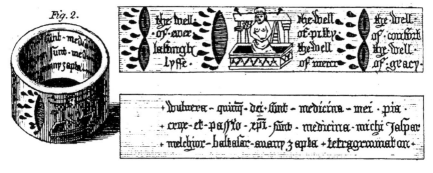

Fig. 6: The Coventry ring.

Fig. 7: The national arms of Portugal, incorporating the Five Wounds.

Fig. 8: Remnants of the Five Wounds in the frieze at Cefntilla, Llandenny. The pierced Feet are surrounded by a Crown of Thorns and set on a shield.

Fig. 9: A late medieval chest panel, Bedwelty Church, Gwent. A Crown of Thorns surrounds the pierced Heart, Hands and Feet.

Fig. 10: A late medieval chest panel, Coety Church, Glamorgan. A Crown of Thorns encircles the pierced Heart (set on a cross flory), Hands and Feet.

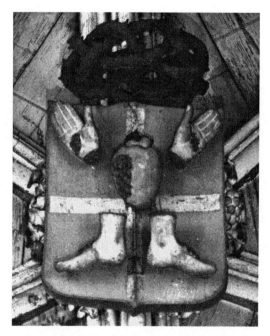

Fig. 11: Roof boss, Winchester Cathedral. The pierced Heart set on a cross, between the Hands and Feet, surmounted by a Crown of Thorns.

Fig. 12: Roof boss, St Tudno's Church, Llandudno. The pierced Heart set on a cross flory, between the Hands and Feet.

Fig. 13: Rood screen panel, Llanengan Church, Co. Caernarfon. The Heart, a Crown of Thorns, the Hands and Feet and three Nails.

Fig. 14: Roof boss, Llan-rhos Church, Co. Caernarfon. Akin to that at St Tudno's church, Llandudno.

Fig. 15: Bench-end, North Cadbury Church, Devon. Mounted on a spear, the pierced Heart and Crown of Thorns are between the Hands and Feet.

Fig. 16: St David's Cathedral, stone carving on a screen behind the Trinity altar. An angel bears a shield displaying the Five Wounds.

Fig. 17: The Shrine of St Margaret Mary, Paray-le-Monial, France.

Fig. 18: Sacred Heart statue, St John's Parish Church, Six Bells.

Fig. 19: Tapestry, St John's Church, Six Bells.

CHAPTER FIVE

AN EXPRESSION OF CHRISTIAN UNITY

An acute realisation of the significance of the Sacred Wounds of Christ in the work of our redemption is shared by all the major Christian Churches. Many of those Christians of the Anglican and Orthodox persuasions, and practically all of the Nonconformist tradition, would not be accustomed to devotions to the Five Wounds as such; they would not, for example, kneel before a crucifix to say prayers relating to each of the Five Wounds.

That does not mean that their understanding of, and their gratitude to Christ for, all His wounds achieved on their behalf is any the less abundant or sincere. In the quest for Christian unity, the varying traditions of the several parts of Christ's universal Church must be respected, indeed treasured. This is the more easily accomplished if union is seen as the coming together of differing denominations rather than the submission of one to another.

So far as the Orthodox tradition is concerned, Lev Gillet pointed out that 'the Eastern Church avoids realistic and bleeding representations of the crucified Lord ... the Eastern pictures of the Cross, like those of the primitive basilicas, represent a crucified Christ, but a Christ crowned and glorified'. The theme of the Cross is much to the fore, for every year the Orthodox Churches keep no less than three feasts of the Cross, and after each Eucharist the faithful kiss a cross held before them.

Moreover, mention of the Wounds is not absent from Orthodox hymnology and writings and, indeed, the Orthodox claim St John Chrysostom as their own. 'Grant me to cling to thy Side', occurs in the hymn written by a Syrian, Romanus the 'Singer' (*d.* 556), in honour of St Thomas. Centuries on, Nicholas Cabasilas (*b.* 1322), a Byzantine mystical author and a nephew of an archbishop of Thessalonica, wrote that in the Lord's Supper we appropriate 'the holy wounds, the bruises and the death of Christ'.

Not unnaturally, the followers of the 19th-century Oxford Movement within the Church of England were more akin to Roman Catholic tradition. Early Anglo-Catholics did not hesitate to include in their manuals of devotion 'Prayers on the Five Wounds of Jesus' taken from the *Paradise of the Christian Soul* translated by Fr Pusey (1800–1882) and others. A notable sermon on 'The Wounds of Jesus' was preached at Swavesey Church, Cambridgeshire, in 1878, by the Vicar, the Revd. Henry Isaac Sharpe (*Appendix 4*). It was preached again there on Good Friday 2003 by the present incumbent, the Revd. John-David Yule. A reflective book was written in 1906 by the Revd. C.G. Clark, rector of St John's, Barbados; entitled *The Refuge of the Sacred Wounds* it included many telling passages, such as:

> The pierced Feet made a special propitiation for the straying feet of the world'.
> The Hands of Jesus have found their last earthly task; they are lifted up above the Head, like the hands of Moses on Horeb, to turn the tide of life's battle, but there are no Aaron and Hur to uphold the weary arms ... but those throbbing painstruck hands are pouring forth ... the ransom price of immortal souls.

Many references to the Five Wounds and the Precious Blood are to be found in *Hymns Ancient and Modern*, for the

Oxford Movement was one of the influences leading to its
compilation and then, later on, in the *English Hymnal*. One
notable hymn writer and translator was John Mason Neale
(1818–1866), who for his religious beliefs and practices
incurred for a lengthy period episcopal displeasure. His
influence in hymnology remains very much alive today,
and amongst his verse comes lines suggesting the wounds
of Jesus as sign-posts on our way to heaven:

> Hath He *marks* to lead me to Him,
> If He be my Guide?
> In His feet and hands are *wound-prints*,
> And His side.   (*EH*, n. 366)

   One of the most notable Anglo-Catholic hymns relating
to the Five Wounds was the work of Father Andrew
(Ernest Hardy, *d.* 1946), founder of the Anglican Society
of the Divine Compassion and the first Anglican cleric to
be ordained (in 1895 at Peterborough) in religious habit
since the Reformation. He wrote:

O dearest Lord, thy sacred head	O dearest Lord, thy sacred feet
With thorns was pierced for me;	With nails were pierced for me;
O pour thy blessing on my head	O pour thy blessing on my feet
That I may think for Thee.	That they may follow Thee.
O dearest Lord, thy sacred hands	O dearest Lord, thy sacred heart
With nails were pierced for me;	With spear was pierced for me;
O shed thy blessing on my hands	O pour thy Spirit in my heart
That they may work for Thee.	That I may live for Thee.

(A and M Rev. n. 436)

   The *Cuddesdon Office Book* (1961 edn), the breviary of
the students of that leading theological college, contains a

prayer adapted from the works of Richard Crawshaw (1613–1649) and others. Crawshaw was very much a High Church Anglican, and friend of Nicholas Ferrer of Little Gidding, though in 1644, with the advent of the Presbyterian Commonwealth, he left England and became a Roman Catholic. The prayer goes:

Jesus, by your wounded feet   Jesus, by your crown of thorns
   guide me through this   annihilate my pride.
   life.

Jesus, by your nailèd hands   Jesus, by your broken heart
   use mine for deeds of   fill mine with love for you.
   love.

Jesus, by your piercèd side
   cleanse my desires.

Devotion to the wounded Saviour was not a preserve of the High Church Movement; it also stemmed from the Evangelicalism of the 18th century. It thus features in the hymnology of William Cowper (1731–1800), a lay assistant to the sailor-turned-priest, the Reverend John Newton. Cowper had known long periods of depression and delusions, and even a spell in what was then unfortunately called a 'lunatic asylum', but later on he was able to write words such as:

> There is a fountain filled with Blood,
> Drawn from Emmanuel's veins . . .
> E'er since by faith I saw the stream
> *Thy flowing wounds supply*,
> Redeeming love has been my theme,
> And shall be till I die.   (*EH*, n. 332)

Cowper's mentor, John Newton, was an Evangelical with Calvinistic leanings. Taking an extreme Calvinist position in the 18th century was another Anglican cleric, the Reverend Augustus Montague Toplady (1740–1778).

Famous for his lines, which tie up well with medieval thought: 'Rock of ages, cleft for me, let me hide myself in Thee', he also penned further on this earlier Catholic theme – that of sheltering in the Wounds of the Lord:

> Like Noah's dove, no rest I find,
> But in thy ark of peace;
> Thy Cross, the balance of my mind;
> *Thy Wounds, my hiding-place*
> > (*Oxford Book of Christian Verse*)

Words which show reliance on the saving nature of the Five Wounds, expressed by Christians of widely differing denominations but with real and sincere devotion.

In the preaching and hymnology of early Non-conformists in Wales, like the itinerant preacher Howell Harris (1714–1773) and the hymn-writer William Williams, *Pantycelyn* (1717–1791), the Precious Blood and the Sacred Wounds featured prominently. Harris was 21 years old when he had a 'conversion' experience, being much affected by the preaching of the vicar of Talgarth, the Reverend Pryse Davies. Harking back to this event a few years later, Harris said: 'I came to see myself, fell at His feet, was made willing, *saw Him bleeding on the Cross*, afterward was sealed'.

It was the start of a very notable ministry, though Howell Harris did not always find favour with the populace he visited. When staying once, early in his ministry, at Tre-hywel, Llanfyrnach, Pembrokeshire, he wrote in his *Diary* (Cambrian News Press, 1966): 'Tis reported for truth here that I am a sheep stealer. I am wounded in my friends house'. Malicious gossip saw him quote the same words which Zechariah had prophesied of his Lord.

Harris told (in 1743) how he began to be more habitually affected with Christ's Blood and Wounds – this, some five years after his conversion experience. In 1741, he had preached on the broken heart at Prendergast, Pembrokeshire, to some hundreds and at Tre-haidd, Nevern, to about 7,000 or 8,000. The prophecy of

Zechariah played a great part in his sermons, especially Chapters 12 and 13 with their references to the Sacred Wounds. In 1750, at Solfa, he wrote that at Tregrove, he had 'more freedom than ever on the Mangled Body, Wounds and Death of the Saviour'. The same year, at Erwd (Breconshire), he 'discoursed on "They overcame by the Blood of the Lamb", and came down strongly on "opening the wounds"'.

As for those who exhibited unusual manifestations during the powerful preaching of the Welsh Methodist Revival, Harris commented that they could not help crying out, some on seeing that they were lost, and others on seeing that they had pierced the Son of God by their sins. As for Harris himself, his epitaph in Talgarth Church tells how: 'Looking to Jesus Crucified, he rejoiced to the last that death had lost its sting'.

Preaching the Blood of Christ was also to the fore in the ministry of William Williams – best known for his 'Guide me, O thou great Jehovah'. He also penned verses such as:

> Let each Drop of blood divine,
> Each Wound be, and each Pain,
> The Contemplation of my Thoughts,
> And ever so remain.
>
> (*Gloria in Excelsis*, 1772)

> Beneath thy Cross, here Jesus, I shall ever stay
> and spend my longing Hours away,
> Think on thy bleeding Wounds and Pain,
> and contemplate thy woes again.
>
> (*Gloria in Excelsis*, 1772)

> And as they contemplate His pains,
> Study His bitter wounds,
> Their knowledge grows, their love inflames,
> Their fervour more abounds.
>
> Faith in his dying wounds,
> The fear of death abates,
> And pure contentedness
> Immediately creates.
>
> (*Songs of Praise*, 1759)

Another Nonconformist writer, who was proud to proclaim himself as a 'Free Church Minister', Edward Shillito (1872–1948), dwelt on the marks of the Passion with which Jesus entered into glory, writing, in his poem 'Jesus of the Scars':

> The heavens frighten us, they are too calm;
> In all the universe we have no place.
> Our wounds are hurting us; where is the balm?
> Lord Jesus, by thy Scars we claim Thy grace.
>
> If when the doors are shut, Thou drawest near,
> Only reveal those hands, that side of thine,
> We know today what wounds are, have no fear;
> Show us Thy Scars, we know the counter-sign.
>
> The other gods were strong, but Thou wast weak,
> They rode, but Thou didst stumble to a throne,
> But to our wounds, only God's wounds can speak,
> And not a god has wounds, but Thou alone.
>
> *(Masterpieces of Religious Verse)*

A striking Nonconformist testimony to the efficacy of the Five Wounds.

CHAPTER SIX

THE SACRED HEART

Enough has been said to show that in the late Middle Ages, the Wound in the Side became increasingly equated with the heart of Jesus, even though the two were very probably not physically coincidental. But, as in popular imagination it is the heart of a person which encompasses all their feelings; the correlation is not surprising. In late medieval and Tudor shields displaying the Five Wounds the heart was placed in the centre, replacing the simple gash of the Wound in the Side. Similar imagery decorated the pectoral cross of Bl. Thomas Beche, the martyred last Abbot of Colchester (1539).

Medieval representations of the Sacred Heart appear at Great Malvern Abbey (in a window), at St John's, Glastonbury (on a cross), and in the private chapel of Abbot Islip of Westminster. In the Brudenell Chapel of Deene Church, Northamptonshire, is a stone reredos dated 1635, with the Sacred Heart carved on the central panel. It is not known whether the reredos reflects Laudian tendencies, or whether it came from the private chapel of the 1st Earl of Cardigan, who was a Roman Catholic.

St John of the Cross (1542–1591) spoke of the true way in which we should see the Sacred Heart, as a vivid symbol of Christ's sacrificial love for us; love which caused Him to die for our sakes. John of the Cross was a Spanish Carmelite friar who, with St Teresa of Avila, tried to reform his Order. Some less observant Carmelites didn't like it; they locked him up for six months in a small monastery cell, and flogged him brutally. He managed to escape, but he knew what it was to suffer for conscience's sake. He wrote a classic work on the *Spiritual Canticles*, in which he saw God as 'wounding us in love', and as giving us wounds of love, which burn us up with immense torment and yearning to see God. John of the Cross also wrote a fine poem, of which three verses:

> A lone young shepherd lived in pain,
> Withdrawn from pleasure of contentment;
> His thoughts fixed on a shepherd-girl,
> His heart an open wound of love.
>
> He weeps, but not from the wound of love,
> There is no pain in such a wound,
> However deeply it opens His heart,
> *He weeps in knowing He's been forgotten.*
>
> After a long time He climbed a tree,
> And spread His shining arms,
> And hung by them, and died,
> *His heart an open wound of love.*
> (*Collected Works of St John of the Cross*, 1966)

In other words, Jesus died of a broken heart. It wasn't so much the spear that plunged into His Side that wounded Him; it was rather our neglectfulness of Him, our lack of concern so often for the things of our faith, our rejection of Him whenever we turn our backs on all that is good and true. It was His broken heart of love that caused Him to cry out from the Cross: 'Father, forgive them; for they know not what they do' (Mark 23.34).

The 'broken heart' formed part of the preaching of Howell Harris in 18th-century Pembrokeshire, and doubtless he would have reminded his throngs of hearers that we, too, must be heartbroken – for our own short-comings in the Lord's service, and the indifference of others. We also must be 'cut to the heart' – like the early hearers of the apostles when they realised that they had crucified their Saviour (Acts 2.37). Mrs Alexander, too, realised the significance of the 'broken heart' of Jesus:

When wounded sore the stricken heart
Lies bleeding and unbound,
One only hand, a *piercèd hand*,
Can salve the sinner's wound.

When sorrow swells the laden breast
And tears of anguish flow,
One only heart, a *broken Heart*,
Can feel the sinner's woe.

(A and M Rev., n. 88)

The saint whose revelations have most fostered modern devotion to the Wound in the Side, the Sacred Heart, was Margaret Mary of Paray-le-Monial in Central France, where her body can be seen today (*Fig. 17*). Born in 1647, she had a tough upbringing but, from childhood, felt a vocation to the religious life. Her family wanted her to join the nearby Ursuline Order, and her brother was ready to put up the 600*l.* necessary. (It is a sad reflection that in past times one could often only become a nun if one's family had money; it surely restricted the free choice of the Holy Spirit). Anyway, Margaret Mary refused to join the Ursulines; she had always wanted to join the 'Holy Marys', as the stricter Visitation nuns were then colloquially known.

She became a 'Holy Mary', and from 1673 to 1675 received frequent visions, chiefly of the Sacred Heart but also of Our Lord bearing His Cross and as a mass of wounds and bruises. At first, her fellow nuns didn't like her practise of mortifications beyond their tradition, nor her visions. Indeed, like many holy nuns, she didn't have an easy time in the convent; for example, she hated cheese, but they forced her to eat it. But Margaret Mary won through, even becoming novice mistress, because she had such a burning love of Christ – a love which puts so many tepid Christians to shame today. Her canonisation in 1920 set the seal of the Church's approval on her revelations.

Devotion to the Sacred Heart not unnaturally passed into Anglo-Catholic usage, and indeed formed part of the early ethos of the Anglican Society of the Divine Compassion. At my boyhood church in Newport, we always kept the annual feast of the Sacred Heart and, when in younger days there were times of difficulty in my life, I often turned either to a crucifix I treasure or in prayer to the Sacred Heart.

I remember well one day late in 1951 or early in 1952, when I was stationed at Farnborough during my National Service; I had been on guard duty and patrol all night which overran its time. My boots were filthy, and I didn't have time to clean them before morning parade. As I stood there in the ranks, I prayed hard to the Sacred Heart, and then along came the inspecting officer (who luckily was my immediate superior), with the sergeant-major behind him, his pencil poised to take my name for dirty boots. The officer, however, gave me a knowing smile and passed on without a word; the sergeant-major had to put his pencil away.

In 1971, when I had a threefold ministry – chaplain at St Woolos Cathedral in Newport, chaplain of the Royal Gwent Hospital and priest with special responsibility for St Martin's Church and the Gaer housing estate, I felt the time had come to move on to a parish of my own. I went to see Eryl Thomas, then Bishop of Monmouth, a fine pastor and leader of men. (He died in December 2001, and his Requiem Eucharist in St Mary's Priory Church, Abergavenny, brought back many memories).

The Bishop said to me, 'Go, and look at Six Bells'; an area of Abertillery without a resident priest at the time, and where the new church building was heavily in debt. I saw there, in the sanctuary of St John's Church, a small statue of the Sacred Heart (*Fig. 18*) – its arms outstretched and beckoning; so, I went to Six Bells for over five happy years. I had a very good friend with little money who died in Nazareth House, Cardiff, some ten years ago. Taken on pilgrimage to Lourdes she, unasked, brought back for me a statue of the Sacred Heart; it is near my side as I type these lines.

Particular devotion to the Sacred Heart may seem un-Anglican, but it is perhaps the terminology, and sometimes the gaudy statue, that makes this so. The significance of the Sacred Heart is well expressed in hymns sung happily by countless Anglicans and Nonconformists for two centuries and more. It was the Anglican-cum-Methodist, Charles Wesley (1707–1788), who urged that our hearts, too, should be holy and pure:

> O for a heart to praise my God,
> A heart from sin set free;
> A humble, lowly, contrite heart,
> Believing, true and clean.
>
> A heart in every thought renewed,
> And full of love divine;
> Perfect, and right, and pure, and good,
> *A copy, Lord, of thine.*
> (*A and M Rev.*, n. 325)

During the recent visit of the Archbishop of Canterbury to West Africa, lady parishioners of the Anglican parish of the Sacred Heart in the Diocese of Accra wore dresses emblazoned with its emblem.

A Latin hymn translated by Edward Caswall (1814–1878), an Anglican cleric later a member of the Birmingham Oratory, has also entered the hymnology of several denominations and sees the Heart of Jesus as indeed a refuge for sinners and for the perplexed:

> All you who seek a comfort sure
> In trouble and distress,
> Whatever sorrow vex the mind,
> Or guilt the soul oppress,
>
> Jesus, who gave Himself for you
> Upon the Cross to die,
> Opens to you His Sacred Heart;
> O to that Heart draw nigh.
> (*A and M Rev.*, n. 104)

Also translated from Latin verse, by Sir Henry Baker

(1821–1877), the Tractarian vicar of Monkland, near Leominster, popular in Anglican worship and again seeing the Heart of Jesus as a place of refuge and of shelter, was:

> Jesu, grant me this I pray,
> Ever in Thy heart to stay,
> I am safe when I abide,
> In Thy *heart and wounded side*.
> (*A and M Rev.*, n. 211)

There are so many occasions when Christians not of the Roman Catholic tradition sing fervently of the love of Jesus as exemplified by His Sacred Heart, who would not feel happy with devotions like those of the First Friday of the month, but are utterly sincere nonetheless in their appreciation of the grace and mercy which Jesus showers upon us. Personally, I like the connotation given by Thomas Goodwin, the Calvinist divine who, in his treatise, *The Heart of Christ in Heaven* (1643), saw the Heart of Jesus as being 'the gracious disposition and tender affection of Christ'.

There is plenty of evidence that the scriptural use of the term 'heart' meant infinitely more in Biblical days than one's physical heart – as in the prayer of the first Christians: 'Lord, who knowest the hearts of all men' (Acts 1.24). As Karl Rahner pointed out, our hearts represent the core of our being and, in showing devotion to the Sacred Heart of Jesus, we are expressing our appreciation of much, much more than a physical heart, albeit one that is divine.

If this be so, why do we need statues of the Sacred Heart? It is because our finite minds require to be fixed on imagery. Just as we need to picture white robed beings to remind us of the existence of invisible angels, a representation of the Sacred Heart evokes in us a remembrance of all that Christ did for us in His Passion.

It is, likewise, terminology such as the 'Immaculate Heart' of Mary which would steer many non-Roman

Catholics away from a true appreciation of her pierced
heart, broken with sorrow at the Crucifixion when the
prophecy of the aged Simeon was fulfilled: 'A sword will
pierce through your own soul also' (Luke 2.35). But John
Keble (1792–1866) reminded Anglicans: 'Her very heart
is riven' (*EH* 216), and Fr Faber's (1814–1863) hymn, 'O
come and mourn with me awhile', is also in the *English
Hymnal*, with its lines: 'Her heart is martyred with her
Son's' (n. 111).

It was St Bernard who expressed it well:

> 'Mother, behold your Son'. These words were more painful
> than a sword thrust for they pierced your soul and touched
> the quick where soul is divided from spirit. What an
> exchange! John was given to you in place of Jesus, a disci-
> ple in place of the Master, a son of Zebedee in place of the
> Son of God. These words must have pierced your loving
> heart, since just to recall them breaks our hearts, hard and
> stony though they be.
>
> (*Divine Office, III*, p. 263*)

In a wonderful Victorian hymn, not sung so much nowa-
days, Sir Henry Baker reminded us of the part Mary
played in the Passion of Our Lord:

> And thee He chose from whom to take
> True flesh His Flesh to be;
> In it to suffer for our sake,
> By it to make us free.
> (*A and M. Rev.*, n. 515)

And all Christians know of Mary that:

> She kept all these things in *her heart*
> (Luke 2.51)

CHAPTER SEVEN

THE GIFT OF TEARS

The prophet Zechariah, in words echoed by St John, reminds all Christ's followers that His Five Wounds are not only a matter of academic or cursory devotion, they are to be an object of inward sorrow and deeply felt.

> When they look on Him whom they have pierced, they shall mourn for Him, and weep bitterly over Him.
>
> (Zech. 12.10)

Sentiments which Fr Faber expressed well:

> O come and mourn with me awhile,
> O come ye to the Saviour's side,
> O come, together let us mourn:
> Jesus, our Lord, is crucified.
>
> (*A and M Rev.*, n. 113)

Today, in western society, we don't normally associate tears with grown men; we keep 'a stiff, upper lip', but it was, and still is, very different in Middle Eastern culture. Long ago, in a psalmist's lament describing the captivity of the Israelites in Babylon (604–562 BC), he tells how: 'By the waters of Babylon we sat down and wept, when we remembered Zion'. They were mindful of the holy city of Jerusalem and God's house. (It was a psalm often sung by St Vincent de Paul (1580–1660) whilst a slave). The same emotion characterised St Peter who 'wept bitterly' when thrice he had denied his Lord (Luke 22.62). Nearly two thousand years on, when in 1967 during the Six Day War the Israeli army entered the Old City of Jerusalem, the first thing the soldiers did was to rush to the Wailing Wall and break down in tears.

One afternoon, in about 1977 when I was Anglican Chaplain in Libya, sitting in my church-cum-villa in Tripoli – the windows open because of the heat, I heard a great wailing which went on and off for several hours. I went outside to see what was going on, and I realised that the wailing was coming from a large family home nearby, where clearly someone had just died. Something of the same nature must have taken place in the case of Dorcas and the weeping widows (Acts 9.39).

The Psalms contain numerous references to physical tears. One writer, in exile and taunted by his enemies that God had forgotten him, cried: 'My tears have been my meat day and night, whilst they daily say unto me, "Where is now thy God?"' (Ps. 42.3). Another psalmist, physically exhausted, mentally depressed, and oppressed by *his* enemies, wrote: 'Every night I weep upon my bed, and water my couch with tears' (Ps. 6.6). That psalmist wept more for himself, the other because God was being blasphemed.

Christian sorrow must always have those two elements, sorrow for our sins which were the cause of Christ's Passion, and sorrow because so many people have turned their backs on God and His Church, and have gone their own way. This was the message too of the writers of the longest psalm in the Bible: 'Mine eyes gush out with water, because men keep not Thy law' (Ps. 119.136).

'Weeping' was clearly a spiritual exercise in Old Testament times, and was associated with fasting. The prophet Joel exhorted his hearers: 'Return to me with fasting with weeping and with mourning' (Joel 2.12), and when King Ahasuerus decreed their wholesale slaughter, there was 'great mourning among the Jews with fasting and weeping and lamenting' (Esther 4.3). The moral for Christians is that fasting helps to promote inward contrition.

When Jesus said, 'Blessed are those who mourn', He didn't mean so much those who had lost a loved one, but rather those who were broken-hearted for their own misdeeds and the sins of others. 'Blessed are they,' Jesus went on, 'for they shall be comforted' (Matthew 5.3) – 'you who weep now shall laugh ... in heaven' (Luke 6.21).

Jesus had concern for the bereaved. He raised to life the only son of the widow of Nain, He wept openly at Lazarus's tomb. But when Jesus said 'blessed are those who mourn', and when Isaiah saw Him as coming 'to comfort those who mourn' (Isa. 61.2), the 'mourning' intended was not sorrow on account of bereavement. Jesus made that very plain when He said to the women of Jerusalem: 'Do not weep for me, but weep for yourselves and your children' (Luke 23.28).

Jesus Himself, in His humanity, was given to emotional feelings and outbursts – He knew fear: 'Father, if it be possible let this cup pass from me' (Matthew 26.39); He knew compassion: so He worked the miracles; He knew anger: so He cast the money-changers out of the Temple, and did so in no uncertain manner; and He knew sorrow. When He came over the brow of the Mount of Olives to meet His Passion, and saw in its entirety the holy city, 'He wept over it' (Luke 19.41) – knowing that its people would reject Him, and that one day the Romans would destroy Jerusalem. The original Greek word here for 'wept' means: 'wailing and sobbing'. Jesus, in other words, broke down, the more so because He alone knew what a glorious future the city might have had.

The only emotion not recorded of Jesus is that of joy and laughter. Perhaps that is simply because any record of it has not survived, but might it be that His mission and destiny were too serious for tears of joy? I like the verses I once read:

I walked a mile with
  Pleasure,
She chattered all the way;
But left me none the wiser
For all she had to say.
	I walked a mile with
	  Sorrow,
	And ne'er a word said she;
	But, oh, the things I
	  learned from her,
	When Sorrow walked with
	  me.

(Robert Browning Hamilton, *Along the Road*, 1885)

One there was who wept outside the tomb of her Crucified Master, St Mary Magdalene, and no wonder she
failed to recognise Him with her eyes full of tears. Those
tears must have given way to shouts of joy! Her faithful-
ness had its reward.

> Weep not Mary, weep no longer!
> Now thy seeking heart may rest;
> Christ the heavenly gardener soweth
> Light and joy within thy breast.
> (*A and M Rev.*, n. 556)

The saintly Bishop Thomas Ken, of Bath and Wells, wrote
about 1675: 'O that with Mary Magdalene, I could weep
much, having so much to be forgiven'.

St Augustine (354–430), Bishop of Hippo and an
outstanding spiritual writer, emphasised the need for
inward contrition and wrote in his *Letter to Proba:* 'Inten-
sive prayer means beating on the door of Him to whom
we are praying by long and devout stirring of the heart.
Often this task is carried on more by groaning than speaking, with more tears than breath' (*Divine Office, III*, 666).
He quoted words of the Psalmists:

> 'My groaning is not hid from Thee'
> (Ps. 38.9)

Thou regardest my lamentation; put my tears into Thy
bottle; Are not these things noted in Thy book?
(Ps. 56.8)

St John Climacus (570–649), Abbot of Sinai, pursued the same theme in his celebrated *Ladder of Divine Ascent*. He wrote: 'Groans and sadness cry out to the Lord, trembling tears intercede for us, and the tears shed out of all-holy love shew that our prayer has been accepted'. He went further to stress the importance of contrition throughout our earthly lives:

> The tears that come after baptism are greater than baptism itself, though it may seem rash to say so. Baptism washes off those evils that were previously within us, whereas the sins committed after baptism are washed away by tears.

John Climacus was followed in this vein by St John of Damascus (*c.* 675–749) who numbered tears among the forms of Baptism, and by St Symeon the New Theologian (949–1022) who considered that sins committed after Baptism cannot be forgiven without tears. All in all, as Lev Gillet pointed out, 'the Orthodox East has an important theology of tears'. Not that the need for intense inward contrition, if not physical tears, went unrecognised in the Western Church. Ascribed to St Gregory the Great (540–604) are the words, linking – as in Old Testament days – contrition with fasting:

> O kind Creator, bow Thine ear,
> To mark the *cry*, to know the *tear*
> Before Thy throne of mercy spent,
> In this holy fast of Lent.
>
> (*EH*, 66)

That connection between spiritual sorrow and penance was also foreshadowed in the Psalms: 'I wept and chastened myself with fasting' (Ps. 69.10).

It was said of St Paula of Rome (347–404) who, widowed, migrated to Bethlehem where she had St Jerome for her spiritual director and confidant:

She prayed long and earnestly before the true Cross, kissed the stones on which the body of Jesus had lain, and watered with her tears the dust of the Dolorous Way along which He had carried His Cross.

The Orthodox St John Climacus, also wrote: 'He who has the gift of spiritual tears will be able to mourn anywhere'. In doing so did he coin for the first time the phrase 'the gift of tears' which came to the fore during the Middle Ages, when the Latin Church provided a Votive Mass for the Gift of Tears? One of its prayers went:

Almighty and most merciful God, who to quench the thirst of your people, drew a fountain of living water out of a rock, draw from our stony hearts tears of compunction, that we may be able to mourn for our sins, and win forgiveness for them ...

Throughout the Middle Ages, there are many instances of holy people and mystics giving vent to physical tears, though critics would say that in some cases their tears resulted from pride, or an over-sensitive nature, or a neurotic condition. A few examples must suffice. Bishop Gundolf of Rochester (*d.* 1109), who is said to have meditated greatly on the Passion, put it thus: 'He who died for us bore Five Wounds, we should weep daily five times recalling this'.

One 12th-century writer said that: 'weeping is the proper work of a monk', and several Cistercians of the period were credited with 'the gift of tears'; amongst them Abbots Henry of Tintern and Turgis of Kirkstall who wept copiously when saying Mass.

St Juliana of Liège (1192–1258), an Augustinian sister, fell to weeping each Passion Sunday when the first strains of the office-hymn, *Vexilla regis* ('The royal banners forward go') burst on her ears. The sobbing during Mass of Bl. Mary D'Oignies (*d.* 1213) so distracted the congregation that she would have to leave the church. The Norfolk mystic, Margery Kempe, had such a great

devotion to Our Lord's Passion and His Precious
Wounds, that she 'cried and roared wonderfully' in St
Margaret's Church there, and visiting the relic of the
Precious Blood at Hailes, she 'had loud cries and boister-
ous weepings'.

Some of the foregoing holy people would perhaps
today be thought unstable or psychologically disturbed,
and some of the accounts concerning them may have been
embellished by later well-meaning hagiographers, but
they were 'mourning' in the truest sense.

The Portuguese shepherd, St John of God (1495–
1550), when in middle-age heard one day in the city of
Granada a moving sermon which cut him to the heart and
filled him with remorse for his evil past. He burst into
tears, and ran out of the church into the streets tearing his
hair and calling for mercy. Taken for a madman, he was
locked up. When he calmed down he was released, and
went on to found the Order of Charity, caring for the sick
and the poor.

In much more modern times, the Calvinistic Methodist
preacher, Howell Harris, brought great crowds to tears in
his tours of Wales. For instance, at 'Llangynlles'
(=?Llangynllo, Cardiganshire) one evening in 1739 he
entered in his *Diary* that he preached for three hours with
vast power, and that many hearers wept almost all the
time. Likewise, at Maenchlochlog the next year, many
hundreds listened to him and, again, wept bitterly. The
Welsh Baptist Enoch Francis (*fl.* 1723) 'would hardly ever
preach without tears streaming down his face from love to
God and men'.

In Catholic Ireland, the native-born Methodist
missioner Gideon Ouseley (1762–1839) was also given to
weeping. Iain Murray tells how:

> On one occasion a priest looked out of the church door for
> an overdue wedding party he was expecting. To his
> surprise he saw them kneeling on the road outside, with
> Ouseley also on his knees and tears flowing.
>
> (*Wesley and Men Who Followed*)

The pacifist communities, with Quaker origins, of the Shakers in the United States literally shook when moved during their meetings. They may have moved one step further for, in 1857, Mother Rebecca Jackson of the Philadelphian Shakers noted of a visiting enquirer: 'she was blessed with a weeping spirit, and we both wept under the influence of the same spirit'.

Hymns of the Welsh Tractarians of the mid-19th century talked of weeping in supplication for the departed, and of contrition for the suffering of the Virgin Mary at her Son's Crucifixion. In *Emynau Hen a Newydd* ('Hymns Old and New'), the Reverend Shadrach Pryce, vicar of Ysbyty Ifan in Denbighshire, wrote:

> Pwy yw'r gwr na wylai hefyd
> Wrth fy fyrio ar fawr ofid
> Tyner fam ein Harglwydd Crist?
> Pwy na wylai'n fawr ei alar
> Wrth ystyried y fam hawddgar
> Gyda'I hunig Fab yn drist?
>   (Hymn 121)

(*Who is the man who would not weep by looking at the great worry of the Mother of Christ? Who would not weep at her mourning considering the loveable Mother with her only Son?*)

Fr Sharach was paraphrasing the sentiments of the Stabat Mater:

> Who on Christ's dear Mother gazing,
> In her trouble so amazing,
> Born of woman, would not weep?

Not unnaturally, the explicit mariology of this hymnal, recently quoted by Dr Peter Freeman in the *National Library of Wales Journal*, did not entirely endear it to all Anglicans of the time, nor to the then prevalent Nonconformist spirit of Wales.

Our 'gift of tears' will be the realisation of our shortcomings in the Master's service, our sadness at seeing His

Church and the sabbath day neglected, our concern at the plight of the oppressed and the persecuted in so many lands, our dismay at the growing rates of abortion and of divorce, our utter dislike of the many programmes with bad language and morals on the television; if such feelings are true of us, and if we try to do something about it, we will be indeed numbered amongst those 'who mourn'. In particular, when we fast in Lent and on Fridays, and when we practise auricular confession – be it general or private – that is a sign of being along the right lines. 'The sacrifice of God is a troubled spirit; a broken and contrite heart, O God, you will not despise' (Ps. 51.17).

One who did think in this vein was Thomas Collins, Superintendent of the Durham Methodist Circuit when (on 9 September 1842) he wrote in his diary:

> I bewail the unbelief of Coventry. There is much poverty and more sin: much degradation and desperate wickedness ... Many read infidel books, gather in infidel assemblies, and answer rebuke with infidel flippancy. I bewail the lack of family care: parents neglect, children run riot, and neither pray. I bewail the strifes of Coventry: in business, in politics, in religion. O Thou, who didst weep over Jerusalem, give me tears for the sins of this people ...
>
> (*Wesley and Men who Followed*)

And, once more, we are indebted to Mrs Alexander:

> Give us hands to work, and *eyes to weep*,
> And hearts to love Thee more.
> (*A and M Rev.*, n. 323)

CHAPTER EIGHT

THE STIGMATA

There have been, and perhaps still are, those people whose intensity of devotion to the Passion of Christ has been such that they have been rewarded with sharing it in a real and physical sense, those we call the stigmatics, those who bear or have borne the stigmata; those in whose hands, feet and side have appeared bleeding wounds; wounds which are more than symbolic of the Wounds of Christ, wounds which cause pain and weakness but also great joy, wounds which are beyond human explanation, wounds which can bleed appreciably (especially on Fridays) but then sometimes disappear and leave no trace. Sometimes the wounding is invisible, producing no exterior effects on the body. St John of the Cross (1542–1591) saw the stigmata as *quasi*-sacramental; an outward sign of inward love for the Five Wounds.

It is possible, but only just possible, that when St Paul wrote: 'I bear on my body the marks of Jesus' (Gal. 6.17) or, in the New English Bible translation: 'I bear the marks of Jesus branded on my body', that he might have meant the stigmata, but more likely he was referring to the results of his several physical beatings, and also there may well be a less literal interpretation of that Pauline saying. Equally, when St Bernard, preaching in 1148 at the funeral of the Cistercian Humbert of Igny, said that the late abbot 'bore the stigmata of Jesus on his body', it may have been a metaphorical allegory to the labours and problems which Humbert had endured.

Not all those who claimed them have, in fact, borne the stigmata, but the condition of those mystics and saints where there are reasonable grounds for believing their wounds to be genuinely supernatural, was often accompanied by prolonged periods of severe ill-health and, sometimes, by visions and other supernatural manifestations such as bilocation, levitation and telepathy. Even in cases where the wounds were not genuine but arose from self-infliction or self-delusion, it does not necessarily follow that those who claimed them were anything other than holy people, devoted to the Lord and mindful of the Wounds He suffered.

There have been many who are dubious regarding the authenticity of the stigmata in some instances. These critics (within the Roman Catholic Church as well as outside it) would ask why were there no known stigmatics before around 1224, why this favour has been granted mostly to women and but rarely to men, why two-thirds of reported stigmatics have come from Italy alone; why, in some instances, the recipients shrink from a proper examination, why the wounds appear in the palms of hands rather than in the wrists where it seems certain the nails were actually hammered, and why the nail marks appear to be round whereas in fact they were probably square? Could invisible stigmata be arthritic pains in the hands and feet? Even the eminent Jesuit, Fr Herbert Thurston, commented that 'in hardly a single case is there not evidence of the previous existence of nervous disorders before the stigmata developed'.

Of the 330 alleged instances of stigmata over the centuries, the first substantial recorded case was that of St Francis of Assisi who, according to his biographer, St Bonaventure, received his wounds during a vision on Mount Alvernia, about the Feast of the Exaltation of the Holy Cross (14 September) in 1224, two years before his death. His marks were not wounds that bled, but impressions of the heads of the nails, round and black, standing clear from the flesh. Fr Thurston, who accepted the genuineness of St Francis's stigmata – 'they could not have been self-inflicted, either consciously or unconsciously', mentions the pessimistic view of J. Merkt (of Tübingen University) who thought them little more than discoloration of the skin, and asserted that St Francis received them only a few days before his death (3 October 1226).

St Bonaventure may have adopted some hagiographical embellishment in his account of St Francis's stigmata – but they were a major cause in promoting devotion to the Five Wounds and leading some people of great piety to believe, rightly or wrongly, that they too bore the marks. The medieval Church set its seal of approval on St Francis's wounds when Benedict XI (1303–1304) instituted the Feast of the Stigmata of St Francis, henceforth observed on 17 September. It was whilst keeping this feast day that Padre Pio first received his wounds. The Anglican Church in Wales, in its propers for St Francis's Day (4 October) prescribes as the Epistle the portion from Galatians containing the words: 'I bear on my body the marks of Jesus' (6.17). It was on this day that, in 1237, Bl. Helen, a Dominican sister of Veszprem in Hungary, received a mark in her right hand and later the wound in the side.

Fr Thurston pointed out that there is some evidence that by the time St Francis received the stigmata, people's thoughts were much occupied with the wounds of the Saviour 'and took them upon themselves'. He mentions the instances of Robert, Dauphin of Auvergne (*c.* 1210–1220) – a case of self-infliction, and of Bro. Dodo, a Frisian Premonstratensian, whose wounds – which *might* have been genuine stigmata – were discovered after his death in 1231, but could have preceded 1224. He also cites the case of a young man – of the English Home Counties seemingly – who claimed to be Christ and procured men to nail him to a cross so that he did display the Five Wounds. At a synod at Oseney near Oxford in

1222, held by Archbishop Stephen Langton, he was sentenced to be immured for life at Banbury on bread and water. Fr Thurston commented that whether he was a fanatic or an impostor did not matter, but that the earlier date of 1222 did.

Medieval stigmatists of note included the visionary St Lutgarde of Aywières (1182–1246). If Thomas Merton – who took a less critical view of the stigmata phenomenon than did Fr Thurston – is correct, then when she was twenty-eight years old and meditating on the martyrdom of St Agnes, Lutgarde only once exhibited the wound in the side – though the scar remained. If this account is chronologically true, then Lutgarde received her mark in about 1210, well over a decade before St Francis received his stigmata. She was a typical stigmatist – resented by some of the other nuns, she endured physical trials – not least going stone blind eleven years before her death, and on one Whit Sunday experiencing levitation during Terce when her body rose 'two cubits' into the air.

Fr Thurston, who rightly said that each case needs to be examined and judged on its own merits, also cites other examples of medieval and later stigmatists and quotes Abbot Philip of Clairvaux (1262–1273), who told how he and other abbots saw blood spurting from the wounds of an ecstatic, Elizabeth, a Cistercian nun of Herkenrode near Liège, but Fr Thurston suggests that she may well have unintentionally maltreated herself during a trance. On rare occasions, such as Good Friday in 1266, Elizabeth exhibited the marks of the Crown of Thorns.

A crown of thorns sensation (feeling prickles) was also experienced by St Catherine of Siena (1347–1380), a Dominican tertiary and a very energetic woman, during the last seven years of her life. At much the same time, she also received the stigmata but as interior feelings of pain. However, Butler's *Lives of the Saints* puts it: 'her wounds were apparent to herself alone during her life, but clearly visible after her death'.

Modern stigmatics have included the Franciscan Sister Veronica Giulani (1660–1727), whom the Ramsgate Abbey *Book of Saints* (1989) describes as having been in a state of almost continual supernatural vision, but a most practical and level-headed religious. She received the five wounds at the age of thirty-seven; her later post-mortem revealed 'a very considerable curvature of the right shoulder, which bent the very bone just as the weight of a heavy cross might have done'. Anne Catherine Emmerich, a German Augustinian nun, received the wounds in 1812 and, it is said, found it difficult to eat and fasted for long periods. There have been critics of the authenticity of her wounds.

A noted example of stigmatism was the case of Therese Neumann (1898–1962), who was given to alternate bouts of convulsions, blindness, deafness, mutism, paralysis and so on. Thomas Merton emphasised that 'one of the fortunate accidents of World War II was that many American Catholics got to see her with their own eyes', but a Professor Martini who examined her observed that blood would only flow from her wounds when he was persuaded to leave the room.

Others in recent times to display such wounds have included Marthe Robin (1902–1981), originally a shepherdess at Drôme near Lyon, and who co-founded the Foyers of Charity. In England, Dorothy Kerin (1889–1963) – the Anglican founder of the Burrswood Fellowship and Healing Ministry, had mystical experiences and received the stigmata following a period in which she was deaf, blind and semi-conscious. Heather Woods, a 43-year old Lincolnshire widow, received the marks in 1992, and talked of receiving messages from long departed people. In the United States, that same year, Fr James Bruse claimed to have Christ's wounds, and that statues in his church in Washington DC, wept in his presence, but when he moved to a rural parish in Virginia, the manifestations ceased.

The most notable modern stigmatic was Padre Pio, who

died in 1968 aged eighty-one. Fr Thurston commented that there was no question but that from September 1918 Padre Pio bore on his body the five wound-marks of the Saviour but, two or so years later, the Congregation of the Holy Office declared that his wounds were not supernatural. He was attributed with the power of bilocation, but doubters have argued that as he always covered his wounds with mittens – none could see them to be sure they were genuine. A doctor, Luigi Romanelli, however, asserted that he had put his hands in Padre Pio's wounds and that his side wound spilt two ounces of blood a day. Padre Pio has been one of the most popular religious figures of the twentieth century, and his grave in the remote village of San Giovanni Rotondu attracts some seven million pilgrims a year, more people than make it to Lourdes. In a *volte-face* by the Vatican, Padre Pio was recently canonised to popular acclaim.

Apart from purely supernatural origins, various other causes for stigmata have been propounded, leaving aside self-infliction. It is thought that in some instances they are psychosomatic, the result of intense prayer and mystical experiences, and so do not detract from their validity as spiritual signs. Where like this, they are genuine, then they are indeed what Redmond Mullin calls 'manifestations of holiness', and a sign of true communion with the Passion of Christ. Fr Thurston, likewise, suggested that the stigmata might easily be produced by purely pathological conditions, given a subject whose thoughts were almost uninterruptedly concentrated upon the marks of our Saviour's Passion.

Throughout the centuries, there have been several well-established cases of fraud. St Magdalena de la Cruz, a Franciscan nun of Cordova in Spain (in 1546) and Sister Maria de la Visitacion, a Dominican nun of Lisbon (in 1588), both allegedly displayed the stigmata, but both were condemned by the Inquisition as impostors – though it has been suggested that neither received a fair hearing. The claims of the English stigmatic, Teresa

Higginson of Bootle (*d.* 1905), were, in retrospect, under-mined by allegations regarding her private life; Berthe Mrazek, a Brussels-born circus performer turned stig-matic, was arrested for fraud and committed to an insane asylum in 1924. Ted Harrison, who has made a special study of the subject both in print and on television, recalled personally seeing five instances of stigmatics where the wounds had been self-inflicted, although the persons concerned might have been quite unaware of the fact.

There is room for debate in the matter of the stigmata, but 'there is no smoke without fire'. Some holy people would indeed seem to have received them as part of God's plan; in others they may have resulted from natural pathological conditions – though in large measure due to a lifestyle of austerity and deep devotion. In other instances, perhaps not many, they were fraudulent.

For ourselves, we are unlikely to be chosen to bear the marks of the Five Wounds, but those who suffer for Christ's sake, like those held for many years in prison cells in China, or those who because of their Christian beliefs lose promotion and employment under other totalitarian régimes, or those in this country who are ridiculed and demoted because they stand up for Christian ethical and moral values, in a lesser but real way are, like St Paul, 'bearing on their bodies the marks of the Lord Jesus'. As the *Stabat Mater* puts it:

> Mother, if my prayer be granted,
> Those five wounds of His implanted,
> In my breast I fain would see.

APPENDICES

1. Extracts from the 'Second Sermon on the Passion', in the Second Book of *Certain Sermons or Homilies Appointed to be Read in Churches*, (1563–71; London, 1676 edn.).

Call to mind, O sinful creature, and set before thine eyes, Christ crucified. Think thou seest His Body stretched out in length upon the Cross, His head crowned with sharp thorns, and His hands and His feet pierced with nails, His heart opened with a long spear ... O my brethren, let this image of Christ crucified, be always printed in our hearts, let it stir us up to the hatred of sin, and provoke our minds to the earnest love of Almighty God. ... Let us trust to be saved by His Death and Passion ... to be partakers of that immortal and everlasting life which He hath purchased unto us by vertue of His bloody wounds ...

2. From an account of a sermon delivered by Daniel Rowland, the notable and magnetic Evangelical parson of Llangeitho, at Nancwnlle (Nantcwnlle), Ceredigion, in November 1756:

Rowland cried out with a most powerful voice, 'Praised be God for keeping the Jews in ignorance respecting the greatness of the Person in their hands. Had they known who He was, they would never have presumed to touch Him, much less to drive nails through His blessed hands and feet, and to put a crown of thorns on His holy head. For had they known they

would not have crucified the Lord of Glory'.
(Eifion Evans, *Daniel Rowland*, Edinburgh, 1985)

3. A Prayer of Bishop Ken (about 1675):

Gracious Lord, look on me, as Thou didst on Peter; and let Thy compassionate look so pierce my heart, that I may weep bitterly for my sins.
   (From 'An Act of Contrition' in his *Manual of Prayers* for the use of the Scholars of Winchester College)

4. Extracts from a very lengthy sermon preached in Swavesey Church, Cambridgeshire, on the evening of Wednesday in Holy Week (17 April) 1878, by the vicar, the Revd Henry Isaac Sharpe. See www.honeyhill.org/wounds.html for the complete sermon.

The Wounds of Jesus

Wounds speak more forcibly than words. The wounds of the soldier, as he lies swathed in his blood on the battlefield, tell the tale of his brave deeds far more forcibly and far more eloquently than the most splendid speech that can be made in praise of him. And there are no wounds so eloquent as the Wounds of Jesus ... In the text Jesus is held up before us, not merely as *wounded*, but as wounded *in the house of His friends* ... The wounds of friends are the most grievous wounds of all.
   ... I look at the Hands of Jesus, and I behold them stabbed through with nails ... And then I look at my own hands ... and I think how often these hands of mine have wrought out my own self-will ... the Hands of Jesus are there on the Cross, and our hands are left at liberty; and what shall we do with them? Jesus Himself tell us: 'Reach hither thy finger, and behold My Hands, and reach hither thy hand and thrust it into my Side, and be not faithless but believing.'
   ... I look at the Feet of Jesus, and I see the iron nail tearing the flesh ... Then I look at these feet of mine, and remember that we all like sheep have gone astray ... our feet have taken us out of the way ...
   ... I look once more, and this time I see the riven Side of Jesus,

and through the gaping wound I seem to look on further still, into His broken Heart ... And I her the bleeding voice of Jesus say, '... O my Father ... from my own broken Heart, which the spear has touched, let the water and the blood flow forth that shall wash away the stain of the sinner's guilt, that he may not die but live.'

... My brethren, these are the wounds with which Christ is wounded in the house of His friends. Our hands wound His Hands, our feet wound His Feet, our hearts wound His Heart. Are you going to wound Him tonight? ... by indifference, by going home and thinking no more about Him? ... If you do so, my best wish for you ... is that just as you lay your head upon the pillow, and ere you close your eyes to sleep, you may have a vision – that you see your Crucified Lord standing by your bedside with His Wounds all streaming – and that you may hear Him saying, 'These are the Wounds with which this night I was wounded in the house of My friends.'

EPILOGUE

My interest in the history of devotion to the Five Wounds of Jesus was in part aroused from reading the sermon given in Swavesey Church in 1878, which formed part of papers which came down to a dear and close friend of mine for nearly forty years, Miss Madaline Mary Stapylton. The vicar of Swavesey, the Revd (later Canon) Henry Isaac Sharpe, was her maternal grandfather. Madaline's parents were his daughter (Margaret Mary – I wonder if she was named after St Margaret Mary, it is quite feasible given the sermon), and the Reverend Robert Miles Stapylton, son of a Lancashire barrister. Madaline was always proud of the fact that she was descended from Sir

Fr R.M. Stapylton

Miss M.M. Stapylton

Miles Stapylton, one of the original Knights of the Garter in the mid-14th century. A number of her family have been clergy, not least another Miles Stapylton who was secretary to the redoubtable Bishop Cosin of Durham (1594–1672), a man close to King Charles the First. The Revd Dr Thomas Stapleton, who died at Louvain in 1598, may have been part of the family.

Her father being a parish priest, Madaline knew several changes of address. She was born in Lolworth Vicarage in Cambridgeshire (on 27 March 1899) where Fr Stapylton was vicar from 1895 to 1909; the house survives though now in private hands. The family moved to Whitstone in Cornwall in 1909, to Clifford in Yorkshire in 1917, and then to St Peter's on the Quay in Folkestone. In the mid-1930s Fr Stapylton retired because of ill-health and the family moved to Cambridge. Fr Stapylton was a very definite Anglo-Catholic – visit Lolworth Church for plenty of evidence of that. He, and the family suffered. His 'High Church ways' were not appreciated by a local farmer in Lolworth who for a time managed to deprive the vicarage of its water supply.

At Clifford, Fr Stapylton refused to obey Archbishop Lang of York's request that he discontinue Reservation of the Blessed Sacrament. The Archbishop declined to visit the parish, but did write to Fr Stapylton referring to 'the good work which you are doing'. The 'good work' he did at Lolworth a decade before is evidenced by the copy of Cardinal Gasquet's *English Monastic Life* given to him and signed, in July 1907, by Bro. Philip, S.D.C., and the nineteen 'members of the St Philip's [Plaistow] Ragged Camp, in Memory of Happy Days'.

Madaline never married – for many years looking after her parents, and she was very fond of her brother, Jan. From Clifford days she had a close and life-long friend in Dennis Hutchinson, but marriage was out of the question because of her commitment in her home and, after service in the RAF, Dennis became a Roman Catholic priest – first of the Diocese of Leeds and then of Westminster. It was from Clifford connections, too, that she became a godmother – to Ann Clarke.

Madaline was educated at a boarding school in north London – where she was not happy, and with the other pupils was evacuated to Eastbourne to complete her education during World War I. Back at home she joined the Womens Land Army in April 1916, with her father's blessing but her mother's misgivings – apart from all else she had to wear trousers! Madaline wrote an account of her life in the early days at the Training Centre to which she was sent at Plumtree, a mile out of Bawtry. Not long after arriving, without any previous experience, 'I was provided with a bucket and sat down and milked a cow straight off'. Later, enlisted on a neighbouring farm to help with threshing, it was a 4 a.m. start! The work was hard, but she enjoyed it, and wrote: 'I never had one regret at joining the Land Army'.

Madaline enjoyed outdoor pursuits like tennis, and for several seasons in the 1930s played hockey for Yorkshire. This took her far afield, including a visit to Ireland. She was a keen bell-ringer, ringing in any church her father had which possessed a peal, and a talented organist – a very helpful ability for any daughter of the vicarage. She adored Cornwall – from her Whitston days, and remained in touch with descendants of Fr Robert Hawker of Morwenstow fame. She had many friends throughout her life, to whom she was always exceptionally kind. The present writer remembers with gratitude the very many times over thirty-five years that he was welcomed in her Cambridge home.

At the heart of Madaline's life was her religious practice, this always came first and foremost. In her later years she was a faithful member of St Clement's, Cambridge, and a sure support to the long-time vicar, Dr Cuthbert Keet. An admirer of the Duke of Windsor, she was also a member of the Society of King Charles the Martyr. Well do I remember an occasion, about 1954, when the Cambridge branch held an outdoor procession at

Lolworth, with Fr Ivor Ramsay, then Dean of King's, carrying a relic of King Charles. Madaline was back at Lolworth in 1953 when the Bishop of Huntingdon dedicated the memorial plaque to her father.

After over fifty years of residence in Chesterton Road, Cambridge, Madaline died on 21 January 1992. Her Requiem Mass at St Clement's and the interment at Lolworth adjacent to her parents and dear brother, took place on 30 January – very appropriately, for it was King Charles the Martyr's feast day. The present writer was privileged to deliver the panegyric and to officiate at the burial. By kind permission of the present incumbent of Lolworth, Evensong was sung in Lolworth Church in Madaline's memory, ten years after her passing, on 16 October 2002.

BIBLIOGRAPHY

Anderson M.D., *The Images of British Churches* (London, 1955).

Anglican Episcopal World, No. 117 (Michaelmas, 2003).

Axon W.E.A., 'The Symbolism of the Five Wounds of Christ', *Trans. Lancashire and Cheshire Antiquarian Society* X (1892).

Baring-Gould S., *The Lives of the Saints* (London, 1872–77).

Bateman W., *The Five Wounds of Christ, A Poem by William Billyng* (Manchester, 1814).

Benson R.H., *Book of the Love of Jesus* (London, 1904).

Berlière U., 'Early Devotion to the Sacred Heart', *Pax* (No. 82; 1927).

Beynon T., *Howell Harris's Visits to Pembrokeshire* (Cambrian News Press, Aberystwyth, 1966).

Boulding M., *Marked for Life: Prayer in the Easter Christ* (SPCK, 1995).

Browne C(arleton)., *A Register of Middle English Religious and Didactic Verse* (Oxford, 1916).

Browne H., *Homilies on the Gospel of St John by St Augustine*, II (Oxford, 1849).

Butler-Bowdon W. (ed), *The Book of Margery Kempe* (London, 1936).

Cave C.J.P., *Roof bosses of Winchester Cathedral* (Winchester, 1953).

Clark-Hunt C.G., *The Refuge of the Sacred Wounds: Seven Meditations on the Passion* (London, 1906).

Conran A. (tr), *The Penguin Book of Welsh Verse* (Penguin, 1967).

Constable G., 'Three Studies', in *Medieval Religious and Social Thought* (Cambridge, 1995).

Divine Mercy in my soul, The Diary of Sister M. Faustina Kowalska (English edn, Stockbridge, Massachusetts, 1987).

Duffy E., *The Stripping of the Altars* (Yale University Press, 1992).

Eton J., *Devotion to the Five Sacred Wounds of Our Lord Jesus Christ* (Gant, 1717).

Evans, E., *Daniel Rowland and the Great Evangelical Awakening in Wales* (Banner of Truth Trust, Edinburgh, 1985).

Ferris D., *The Life of St Mary Frances of the Five Wounds* (Dublin, 1878).

Finaldi G(abriel)., *The Image of Christ* (National Gallery, 2000).

Franz A(dolph)., *Die Messe im deutschen Mittelalter* (Freiburg and Breisgau, 1902).

Freeman P., 'The Contribution of some Tractarians in Mid-Nineteenth Century Wales to Welsh Poetry and Hymnology', *National Library of Wales Journal*, XXXII: No. I (Summer, 2001).

Gillet, J(ev)., *Orthodox Spirituality* (London, 1945).

Glemp J. Cardinal, *Poles – We enter now the Twenty-First Century* (Warsaw, 1998).

Gougaud L., *Devotional and Ascetic Practices in the Later Middle Ages* (ed. G.C. Bateman, London, 1927).

Gray D(ouglas)., 'The Five Wounds of Our Lord', *Notes and Queries*, New Series, vol. 10 (No. 208: 1963).

Gray M., *Images of Piety* (British Archaeological Reports, British Series, 316; 2000).

Gray M., 'The Clergy as Remembrancers of the Community', *The Monmouthshire Antiquary*, XVI (2000), p. 116.

Green R.L., *Early English Carols* (2nd edn, Oxford, 1977).

Halliwell J.O., *A Selection from the Minor Poems of Dan John Lydgate* (London, 1840).

Harrison T(ed)., *Stigmata: A Medieval Mystery for a Modern Age* (London, 1994).

H.W.H., *A Manual of Prayers for Young Persons* (und.), amended edition of Bishop Ken's *Manual of Prayers for the use of the Scholars of Winchester College*.

Johnston F., *Margaret Sinclair* (CTS, 1979).

Kavanagh K. and Rodriguez O., *The Collected Works of St John of the Cross* (London, 1966 edn).

Kelly I., 'Apostle of Suffering', *Catholic Times* (30 April 2000), p. 6.

Lewis J.M., *Welsh Monumental Brasses* (National Museum, Cardiff, 1974).

Lewis M(ostyn)., *Stained Glass of North Wales* (Altrincham, 1970).

Lord P., *The Visual Culture of Wales: Medieval Vision* (University of Wales Press, Cardiff; 2003).

Luibheid C. and Russell N., *John Climacus, The Ladder of Divine Ascent* (London, 1982).

MacCracken H.N., *The Minor Poems of John Lydgate*, (London, Early English Text Soc., 1911).

Martin E., 'Religious Belief in Medieval Gwent', *Gwent County History Association Newsletter*, 6 (May 2001).

Sister Mary Martha Chambon of the Visitation of Holy Mary (Chambèry) and the Sacred Wounds of our Lord Jesus Christ (anon., London, 1926).

Merton T., *What are these Wounds?* (Dublin, 1948).

Mullin R., *Miracles and Magic* (London, 1979).

Murray Iain H., *Wesley and Men Who Followed* (Edinburgh, 2003).

National Library of Wales, Badminton Deeds, Group I, no. 1451.

O'Strowan J.K., *The Humble Remonstrance* (London reprint, 1733).

Parry-Jones D., *A Welsh Country Parson* (Batsford, 1975).

Patterson F.A., *The Middle English Penitential Lyric* (New York, 1911).

Penelope Sr., *The Works of William of St Thierry*, I (Shannon, Ireland); Cistercian Fathers Series No. 3; 1971 (Cistercian Publications, Kalamazoo, Canada).

Pope T.A., *A Little Office of the Five Sacred Wounds* (London, 1926).

Raw B.C., 'The Ancrene Riwle', in Rowland B. (ed)., *Chaucer and Middle English Studies* (London, 1974); *Anglo-Saxon Crucifixion Iconography* (Cambridge, 1990).

Rosmini A., *Of the Five Wounds of Holy Church* (ed. H.P. Liddon, London, 1883).

Royal Commission on Historical Monuments (England), *An Inventory of ... London*, II (*West London*; London, 1925).

Ryan J.K., *Introduction to the Devout Life by St Francis de Sales* (London, 1953).

Scarisbrick D., *Jewellery in Britain, 1066–1837* (Norwich, 1994).

Salmond S.D.F., *The Writings of Hippolytus*, II (Edinburgh, 1869).

Scott K., *Later Gothic Manuscripts, 1390–1490*, II (London, 1996).

Scupoli, L(orenzo), *The Spiritual Combat* (London, 2nd edn, 1950).

Seeley M., *The Later Evangelical Fathers* (London, 1914).

Seward D(esmond)., *The Monks of War* (London, 1972).

Sharpe R.R., *Calendar of the Wills in the Court of Husting*, II (London, 1890).

Sheen F(ulton)., *The Life of Christ* (London, 1959).

Shillito E., *Jesus of the Scars and other Poems* (London, 1919).

Sidney, Mary, Countess of Pembroke, *A Poem on Our Saviour's Passion* (London edn, 1862).

Simpson, W. Sparrow, 'On the Measure of the Wound in the Side of the Redeemer', *Jnl. British Archaeological Assocn.*, XXX (Dec. 1874).

Starkey D., *The Inventory of King Henry VIII* (London, 1998).

Stupart G.J. (tr)., *Homilies of St John Chrysostom on the Gospel of St John* (Oxford, 1848–52).

Take the high road, the life of the Venerable Sister Mary Francis of the Five Wounds (anon; Hawarden, 1993).

Thomas D.R., *History of the Diocese of St Asaph*, III (Oswestry, 1908).

Thurston H(erbert)., S.J., *The Physical Phenomenon of Mysticism* (London, 1952).

Walsh M.J., *The Heart of Christ in the Writings of Karl Rahner* (Rome, 1977).

Williams G(lanmor)., *Welsh Church from Conquest to Reformation* (Cardiff, 1962).

Williams R.E., *Called and chosen: the Story of Mother Rebecca Jackson and the Philadelphia Shakers* (London, 1981).

Williams W(illiam)., *Pantycelyn.*, *Gloria in Excelsis, or Hymns of Praise to God and the Lamb* (Carmarthen, 1772).

(Ibid). *Songs of Praises, English Hymns and Elegies* (ed R. Brinley Jones; Drovers Press, Llanwrda, 1995).

Williamson B., *The Bridgettine Order* (London, 1922).